The First Practical Pyramid Book

-THE-
FIRST
PRACTICAL
PYRAMID BOOK

*Free Energy for Beauty, Health, Gardening,
Food Dehydration, and Meditation*

NORMAN H. STARK

SHEED ANDREWS AND McMEEL, INC.

Subsidiary of Universal Press Syndicate

Kansas City

CAUTION TO READERS

In writing the formulas for Beauty and Personal Care and Controlling Garden Pests, I have excluded hazardous materials wherever possible, but in some cases they must be included to make a product effective. In making a formula, the reader should observe any note of caution added at the end of the recipe as well as any special cautions accompanying the ingredients.

We all know that materials such as waxes and oils will burn, so I have concentrated the warnings to materials that may be less familiar. But remember, all chemicals, including ordinary table salt, should be kept out of the reach of children, carefully labeled, and used only for the purpose they are intended.

The value and safety to you of the products in this book depends upon your careful use of the materials shown in the proportions given, as well as your observing any special cautions appearing in the book or with the materials. Neither I nor the publisher can be responsible for the efficacy of the products or your own safety if you do not follow these instructions and precautions.

Library of Congress Cataloging in Publication Data

Stark, Norman.
    The first practical pyramid book.

    SUMMARY: Explains how to use the mysterious electrical energy force existing within a pyramid for such purposes as dehydrating foods, chemically changing water, and sharpening razor blades. Includes instructions for building your own pyramid.
       1.   Pyramids--Miscellanea.   2.   Occult sciences.
[1.   Pyramids--Miscellanea.   2.   Occult sciences]
I.   Title.
BF1999.S718   001.9   77-1574
ISBN 0-8362-0690-8
ISBN 0-8362-0691-6 pbk.

To James H. (Jim) Sargent,
my friend and outdoor companion
of many years

Contents

FOREWORD

Stark Research Corporation was founded in 1940 in the Milwaukee metropolitan area. It was set up to manufacture chemicals, conduct chemical research and develop chemical processes.

One of our early assignments came from the United States government during World War II. It was a contract for making solid fuel, and we successfully developed the formula, built the equipment, and produced millions of pounds of material. Many additional assignments were received and fulfilled successfully up to the end of the war.

My interest never was in manufacturing, so after the military need for materials no longer existed, we converted our efforts to research and development.

Over the years our research and development work resulted in major breakthroughs in both formulas and processes. For example, many years went into the development of a continuous high-speed vacuum process for the impregnation of fibrous materials such as paper with liquid formulations. Typical uses consisted of: waterproofing paper with wax compounds, greaseproofing for butter wrappers, impregnating plastic laminates for use as sink tops, etc. Other major developments included a dielectric mass that was molded into both gas and electric infrared

9

heaters, a chemical method for restructuring the cells of polyurethane foam to make it suitable for use as an air filter, sensing the degree of hardness of water, etc.

Over the years my hobby, in addition to my work, was in developing, modifying, and testing chemical formulas that would enable individuals to make their own chemical products at substantial savings, and would be educational as well. Throughout this period of time we also conducted pyramid research to determine what effect pyramid energy would have on liquids, solids, and the human body.

In the fall of 1973 we compiled about three hundred formulas into a book called *The Formula Manual*. This was purchased by teachers and their students from elementary school through college graduate level and became an immediate success.

The following year we published the second edition of *The Formula Manual,* which was enlarged as well as revised. This, also, was an immediate success.

Each year we have updated and expanded this manual and at the time of this writing the fourth edition, containing almost six-hundred formulas, is about to be published. From the inception of the first edition of *The Formula Manual* through the third edition about eighty-five thousand copies have been sold for educational use.

During the summer of 1975 I met with the principals of Universal Press Syndicate and their publishing subsidiary, Sheed Andrews and McMeel, Inc. They felt that a weekly syndicated feature, based on a formula per week, and a simplified consumer version of the book, would find a market. And how right they were!

In August 1975 my first syndicated column called "The Formula" appeared in newspapers nationally, and met with immediate acceptance from editors and readers alike. At this time it is carried as a regular weekly feature by more than one hundred papers from coast to coast.

In October 1975 *The Formula Book,* a consumer version of *The Formula Manual,* was published by Sheed

Andrews and McMeel, Inc. It became an immediate best seller, with hundreds of thousands of copies sold to date.

The Formula Book 2, published in November 1976, is the second in the series. It, too, became an immediate best seller, and will be followed by additional volumes, each containing new and revised formulas.

The First Practical Pyramid Book which you now hold is the first in a series covering the phenomenon of the pyramids. Its purpose is to provide the lay person with a working knowledge of a pyramid—what it is, what it does, how to construct one, and how to use it.

That an unknown electrical energy force exists within a pyramid has been scientifically recognized. How to identify it has not been. However, we do know that this free energy can dehydrate foods, make yogurt, preserve cut flowers and herbs, reduce the time between planting and harvesting, keep razor blades sharp, help house plants to grow faster and stronger, chemically change water, energize aluminum, and make meditation easier and more effective.

Here at Stark Research we subscribe to the principle that our books should be based on actual experience rather than on theories. Accordingly, we maintain a full-scale research, development, and testing laboratory near Tucson, Arizona, where formulas are made up and tested under actual use conditions. Included in our facilities are pyramids of many sizes including our master unit. This is an exact scale model of the Cheops Pyramid in Egypt. It stands on a base 20 feet x 20 feet and the height is 12 feet from its base to its apex. Orientation is to true north as shown in the drawings in this work.

I want to express my thanks to the many people who have advised and guided me in the writing of this book: Jim Andrews, Donna Martin, Tom Thornton, and their associates at Sheed Andrews and McMeel, John McMeel and Lee Salem of Universal Press Syndicate and their associates, and Dr. Ed Nigh of the University of Arizona.

Special mention must be given to my business partner, Julie Charnis, without whose invaluable help and organizational ability this book would not be what it is.

And last, but certainly not least, there's my wife Eileen. She's a pick. Everything has to be just so or it's "no go." As a registered nurse with a background in nutrition, she took over the responsibility of preparing the foods for drying, supervising dehydration in the pyramid, and selecting the best methods for reconstitution. Since it's a real challenge for me to boil an egg, I don't see how the dehydration section of this book could have been written without her culinary expertise.

We hope you will enjoy this book and put a pyramid to work for you.

—*Norman Stark*

Introduction

The Cheops Pyramid, the seventh wonder of the world, is the tallest of many pyramids found not only in Egypt but in other countries as well. Located about ten miles west of Cairo, it contains over two-and-one-half million blocks of limestone and granite. The amazing fact is, that after thousands of years, these segments still fit together so perfectly that it is difficult to see the lines of demarcation. This suggests that either the ancient Egyptians, or some other culture, had knowledge that we still don't possess, thousands of years later.

It has been estimated that some of the blocks of granite used in the structure weigh as much as 70 tons each and would have had to be transported to the pyramid from the Aswan quarry near Syene, which is five-hundred miles up the Nile. Barges on the Nile? Perhaps. Air transport from another culture? Who knows? At any rate the stones were transported and are there today.

The Cheops Pyramid stands on a man-made plateau that is less than an inch off level after thousands of years. (Doesn't it make you wonder what "they" had that we don't have when our modern highways are full of pits and chuck holes after a couple of years?) The Cheops Pyramid itself is estimated to be less than one inch off of its original level, after thousands of years.

The base of the Cheops Pyramid covers about 13 acres of area. Its height from base to apex (top) is 482 feet. This creates a slope of 51°51′ on the sides. This slope is critical, as will be explained later. Its orientation is to true north, a deviation from magnetic north.

Explorations over thousands of years have established that there are a number of rooms within the Cheops. However, this subject has been well covered in the literature and is not relevant to our discussion of how to use pyramid energy. The area of importance to us is known as the King's Chamber, where the electrical force seems to be the greatest. This room is located below the apex, roughly one-third the distance up from the base to the apex.

The King's Chamber is a bare room thirty feet long, seventeen feet wide by nineteen feet high, containing only a lidless sarcophagus (a rectangular stone coffin). Although we have no first-hand knowledge of it, many students believe that this may have been an initiation place used by such groups as the Knights Templars, Rosicrucians, and others where select scholars were elevated to a higher level of consciousness.

There is a considerable amount of evidence that the Cheops also served as a mathematical and astronomical tool. A mathematician discovered that if the perimeter of the Cheops was divided by twice the distance from base to apex, the result was 3.144 which is very close to Pi, 3.14159+. In other words, the Cheops Pyramid has the unique geometrical property that its height stands in the same ratio to its circumference as the radius to the circumference of a circle. And since Pi was not discovered until many years later, it becomes apparent that the pyramid builders had an advanced mathematical knowledge. It is further postulated that, by this calculation the Cheops Pyramid may have been a model representing the earth's circumference, with the distance from base to apex representing the relationship to the North or South Pole.

The great Library of Alexandria was intentionally destroyed by Christian terrorists about the year 390 A.D. on direct orders from the Christian Emperor Theodosius. Had it not been for this tragic event much information about the Cheops Pyramid may have been available to answer some of the perplexing questions that still exist.

Recent scientific interest in the power of pyramids began when a Frenchman, M. Bovis, entered the Great Pyramid some years ago and found dead animals in the King's Chamber which had not decayed but had instead dehydrated and mummified. Believing that the shape of the pyramid might have significance he built a small scale model of the pyramid and placed a dead cat in it about one-third the distance from the base to the apex, at the King's Chamber level. The cat mummified.

A Czechoslavakian radio and television engineer,

Outside view of pyramid

Karel Drbal, read Bovis's published reports of his research, and performed his own experiments. He concluded that there was definitely a relationship between the shape of the space inside the pyramid and the physical, chemical, and biological process going on inside it.

While reports on Bovis's and Drbal's experiments have provoked much speculation and inquiry into the mysterious power of pyramids, little has been advanced in the way of scientifically validated ways in which pyramids may be put to practical uses. My own interest, then, has been to construct and experiment with pyramids and to share with my readers the bountiful results of harnessing pyramid energy.

1

What Goes On In There?

Well, that's anyone's guess. But when highly qualified scientists from prestigious universities and government and private research groups using the most sophisticated equipment available haven't been able to come up with answers, it would seem presumptuous for us to come up with a theory. But we do have one that may account for at least some answers. Before reading it, however, we ask that you refer to Figure 1, a laboratory report run on water samples for us by the University of Arizona. Both samples are tap water drawn at the same time. Sample #1 was exposed to pyramid energy, while Sample #2 was not.

The symbols in the chart stand for the following chemical elements:

Ca—Calcium
Mg—Magnesium
Na—Sodium
Cl—Chloride
SO$_4$—Sulfate
HCO$_3$—Bicarbonate
CO$_3$—Carbonate
F—Fluorine
N—Nitrogen

As you can see there have been dramatic changes in the composition of the water exposed to pyramid energy. Please note the substantial increase in nitrogen in the pyramid treated sample. Nitrogen is a tasteless, odorless gas that will not support combustion. It occurs in the atmosphere making up about 78 percent by volume and 75.5 percent by weight, and serves to dilute oxygen.

Ammonium salts in soil are converted to nitrates by microorganisms. They are first oxidized to nitrites, and then oxidized to nitrates by bacteria called nitrobacteria.

Nitrogen is also fixed in the form of oxides by electrical forces in the atmosphere where they are transported to the soil in the form of nitric and nitrous acids by rain, and then these acids form nitrites and nitrates in the soil. During a thunderstorm it is estimated that as much as ten tons of nitric acid per hour are produced.

19

Figure 1

THE UNIVERSITY OF ARIZONA
College of Agriculture
Department of Soils, Water and Engineering
Soils, Water and Plant Tissue Testing Lab.
Tucson, Arizona 85721

| ROUTINE WATER ANALYSIS |

COLLECTOR:

Name _Ed Nigh_

Address _Plant Sciences_ _____ Zip _____

DATE _July 10, 1976_

BILL TO:

Name _Stark Research Corp_

Address _4850 N. Campbell Ave._
Tucson, A.z
_299-1374_ Zip _85718_

PO/Fund No. _____

COMMENTS:
_____
_____
_____

Sample Location			ID	Sample Date	Source[1]			Other (Specify)	Well Depth	Static Water Level	Lab. No.	EC x10³	Solu Salts ppm	pH	Milligrams per liter (mg/1)[2]									
Sec.	TWP	R			E	W	G								Ca	Mg	Na	Cl	SO₄	HCO₃	CO₃	F	N³	B	SAR⁴
			#1								2980	0.37	321	8.1	36	8.5	46	20	75	132	2.4	0.18	66	—	1.8
			#2								2981	0.37	396	7.9	102	6.8	38	16	32	200	0	0.16	49	—	1.0

[1] Source: E = Effluent
W = Well
G = Gravity
O = Other (specify)

[2] mg/1 is approximately
equal to ppm

[3] Analyzed as NITRATE

[4] Sodium Absorption Ratio

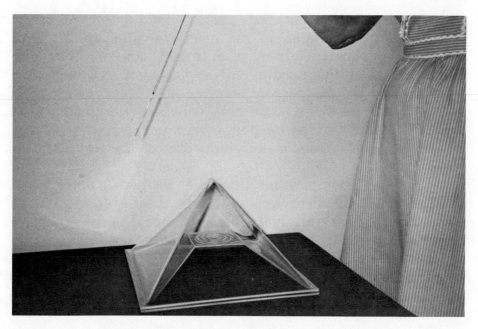

Steel needle swinging over apex of pyramid.

We can see no other possible way by which the nitrogen content of pyramid water can so dramatically be increased other than to feel that a correlation between atmospheric electrical forces and pyramid electrical forces must exist.

Another way by which we can establish that an electrical force exists is by an experiment using a small laboratory pyramid. This must, of course, be an exact scale model of the Cheops, aligned to true north and away from electrical disturbances. If a steel needle attached to a thread is held over the apex, it will slowly start to swing around the apex in a circular motion, which will then turn to an oval path, and finally swing back and forth as a pendulum over the true north/south line.

Now here's a further observation that frankly has me completely stumped. The distance of the swing varies

21

greatly depending on the person holding the thread. Here's another stumper. If the needle swings on a 1 inch arc for the person holding the thread, and another person, for whom the needle will swing over a 3 inch arc, puts a hand on the person holding the thread, the needle will increase its swing. The only conclusion we come to is that there must be some connection between the electrical system of a person's body and that of the force within the pyramid.

They say that pictures don't lie. So here's more proof that an electrical force exists within the pyramid. Kirlian photography is a relatively new science that was developed in Russia. It has the capability of recording on film what can't be seen by the human eye. A good example of this would be an aura surrounding an object such as a pyramid, the human body, or all space that contains electrical energy.

The corona effect (Kirlian) depends on the coupling of high voltage, high frequency A.C. power to the mass to be photographed. The energy shows up as radiation from ultraviolet through visible and infrared light, and in certain parts of the electromagnetic spectrum.

Kirlian photography has now given us a tool to establish conclusively that pyramid energy is not restricted to the confines of the inside of the pyramid alone, but in effect radiates from it as well. (See photo.) Perhaps this is the reason that it is not considered safe to operate aircraft in the vicinity of the pyramids, because numerous instrument malfunctions have been reported by pilots.

As stated earlier, some startling changes in pyramid water have been established. Also, the oscillation of the needle over the pyramid apex has been discussed. Now, when water treated in the pyramid is removed and the needle is held over the top of its plastic container, the action of the needle approximates that of when it is held over the pyramid apex. As far as I'm concerned, this clearly establishes the fact that the pyramid energy has been transferred to the water.

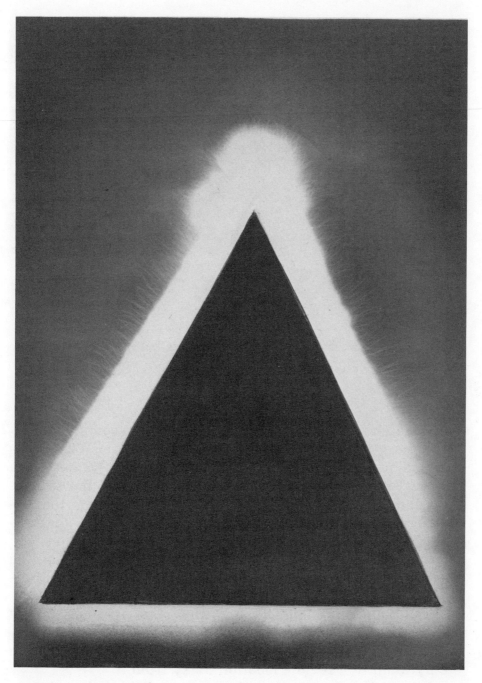

A Kirlian photograph showing energy radiating from the pyramid in the form of an aura

Energizing aluminum plate and aluminum foil in the pyramid

Aluminum also has the capability of becoming a pyramid energy generator. But it can be a fooler. When it is exposed to pyramid energy it takes time for it to adsorb this energy to its capacity. After it has reached the saturation point, it becomes a generator and releases the energy for up to a year, depending, of course, on the volume of the section. Again, proof of the adsorption and release of pyramid energy can be established by holding a steel needle over the aluminum as was done with the pyramid apex and pyramid treated water.

The importance of the fact that the pyramid energy can be adsorbed and released by substances such as aluminum and water is that this energy can be taken from the pyramid to a remote location away from it.

Mummification (embalming) as practiced by ancient Egyptians was an art that is unsurpassed today. Corpses

24

have been found that are thousands of years old and in a perfect state of preservation. In 1963 biologists at the University of Oklahoma determined that the skin cells of a mummy, dead for several thousand years, were capable of sustaining life. That is, a piece of skin can be grafted from a mummy onto a human or animal and the graft will "take." Presumably these mummified bodies were treated in a pyramid which probably accounts for the phenomenon of dehydration.

As we previously stated, no one really has been able to identify the force active in pyramids. However, other than for purely academic reasons, I can't help wondering if it really makes that much difference. After all, if we didn't know an apple was called an apple, it would taste just as good and have the same nutritional value.

2

What Can a Pyramid Do?

The energy force within a pyramid can do many things to benefit all of us.

1. *Meditation* is far easier to accomplish inside a pyramid than outside of it for many people. The Alpha level of mind, where constructive thoughts are born, can be reached more easily by most people, including myself, in the pyramid. The benefits are better physical and mental health and improved material well-being.

2. *Dehydration of vegetables and fruits* such as asparagus, beets, carrots, onions and onion greens, corn, peas, peppers, beans, mushrooms, apples, pears, and peaches with free energy.

3. *Dehydration of meat* such as beef, venison, elk, moose and fish with free energy.

4. *Transferring pyramid energy to water* for medicinal and cosmetic uses.

5. *Transferring pyramid energy to aluminum* for a dozen household purposes.

6. *Making yogurt* in the pyramid with free energy.

7. *Germinating seedlings and growing plants* in the pyramid with free energy.

8. *Mellowing wine* in the pyramid with free energy.

9. *Mellowing tobacco* in the pyramid such as pipe tobacco, cigarettes, and cigars.

10. *Sharpening razor blades* in the pyramid for dozens of extra shaves. (Always align the razor blade with the north-south axis of the pyramid.)

I will explain how to make the pyramid work for you in these ways and many others in subsequent chapters.

3

Building a Pyramid

Anyone who can read a ruler and cut pieces of material can easily build a pyramid. No calculations are required, as the correct angles are automatically built in for you. But there are two basic decisions that must be made before anything else can be done: (A) location, and (B) size.

We strongly recommend that you start with a small size unit for indoor use, and then work up to larger sizes learning from previous experience. Location is of primary importance. The area should be level and as far away from electrical disturbances as possible. Prime offenders are: television sets, radios, including CB, microwave ovens, fluorescent lights and all types of transformers.

Your next step is to establish the orientation of the pyramid you intend to build.

For this step, a compass is essential. We prefer the kind that has a folding post used as a sight. They're inexpensive and available at any sporting goods store.

After you have established a line to magnetic north, your next step will be to call the nearest Federal Aviation Agency Flight Service Station and ask for the deviation of true north from magnetic north. In the Tucson area, where we have built our pyramids, the deviation is 13 degrees to the east.

While deviations vary in different geographic regions, the method of calculation is the same. Let's assume it's 10 degrees east in your area. If magnetic north is 360 degrees, you would subtract 10 degrees, and true north would be 350 degrees.

Now, using your compass, stand at the southernmost point on your magnetic north line and site to 350 degrees. Establish a line to that heading which will be true north. One side of your pyramid must be aligned to that line. Having established this, you're now ready to proceed with the project. (See drawing—Orientation of Pyramid.)

Five things critical to success in the effectiveness of a pyramid are:

1. Selection of materials to be used in its construction.

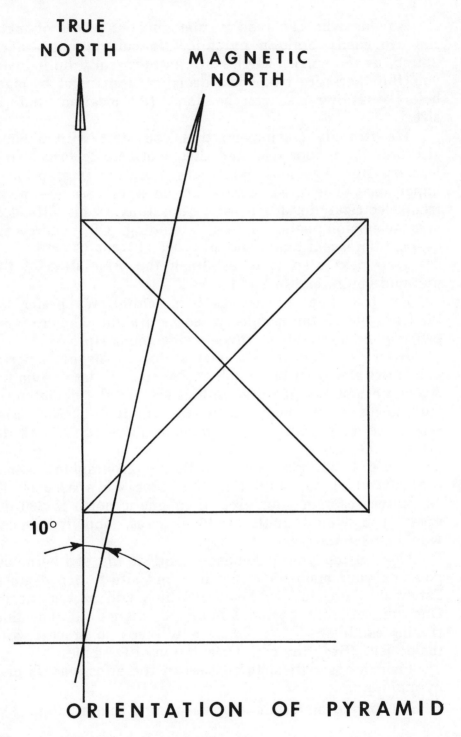

TRUE
NORTH

MAGNETIC
NORTH

10°

ORIENTATION OF PYRAMID

2. The angle of slope from base to apex, known as the apothem.
3. The alignment to true north.
4. The location of the work area within the pyramid.
5. Temperature control if it is to be used for plants.

MATERIALS

A wide range of materials can be used in the construction of a pyramid. Our preferences are: cardboard, wood, plastics, glass, fiberglass, canvas, or anything nonmetallic. The metallic exception is aluminum, which has interesting characteristics covered in another chapter. Other researchers state that any nonferrous metal may be used, but our tests have not been encouraging.

THE SLOPE ANGLE

The slope angle is highly critical to the effectiveness of the pyramid. It is 51°51' and is the angle between the center line of any face of a pyramid and the same center line of the floor.

ALIGNMENT

The procedures for aligning to true north are found on the previous pages.

LOCATION

While the electrical forces appear to be present in all sections of the pyramid, the greatest area of strength is in the King's Chamber, below the apex, one-third up from the base. The next best area is around the perimeter at the same height. For example, if the pyramid is 12 feet high as our large one is, the workbench area will be 4 feet from the base and 8 feet below the apex.

Internal view of King's Chamber level of pyramid

TEMPERATURE CONTROL

Temperature control is a variable depending on location. In our own experience, temperature has had no effect on the dehydration process, although the humidity of some areas may be a factor. We have successfully dried foods at readings as low as 40° F. and as high as 90° F. with no appreciable difference in time. If, however, the pyramid is to be used for plants, meditation, or health purposes, a moderate temperature should be maintained.

Here in the Southwest desert region, 100° days are common during the summer months. So cooling is our major problem. To meet this need we use an evaporative cooler located on the outside of the pyramid and pass the cooled air inside through plywood duct work.

Conversely, in many areas of the country, the need

for heating is more important than cooling. This can be provided by any heat source such as gas or electricity. But the heating unit, being metallic, should be outside of the pyramid and the heated air conveyed to the inside by nonmetallic or aluminum duct work.

Having selected a level site for your pyramid, removed from electrical disturbances, you'll have to decide on the size that best suits your intended use. We have found that a rule of thumb is to limit the volume of what you put into a pyramid to not more than 5 percent of the internal volume. For example, if you wanted to treat a gallon of water (approximately 280 cubic inches), the volume of space within the pyramid should be at least 5600 to 6000 cubic inches.

Now that you have decided on the size of pyramid to construct, you can begin with your design. We could give you all kinds of dimensions and mathematical formulas, but in all likelihood, they wouldn't cover the exact size you want and would only be confusing. But there is an easy, simple way that does not require any calculation.

Figure 2 is a side view of one section of a pyramid laid out to the exact scale of the Cheops. If you desire to make a larger unit, this drawing may be cut out and used as a templet to trace its shape on the material used. Remember that regardless of size, this same shape will remain as a constant for the apex. The only thing that changes to make the pyramid larger or smaller is the length of the slope lines. The following table makes this an easy choice.

Length of Slope Lines	Pyramid Height	Base Size
107-5/8″	72″	9′5″ x 9′5″
89-11/16″	60″	7′10″ x 7′10″
71-3/4″	48″	6′3″ x 6′3″
53-13/16″	36″	4′8″ x 4′8″
35-7/8″	24″	3′1″ x 3′ 1″
26-7/8″	18″	2′4″ x 2′4″

Figure 2

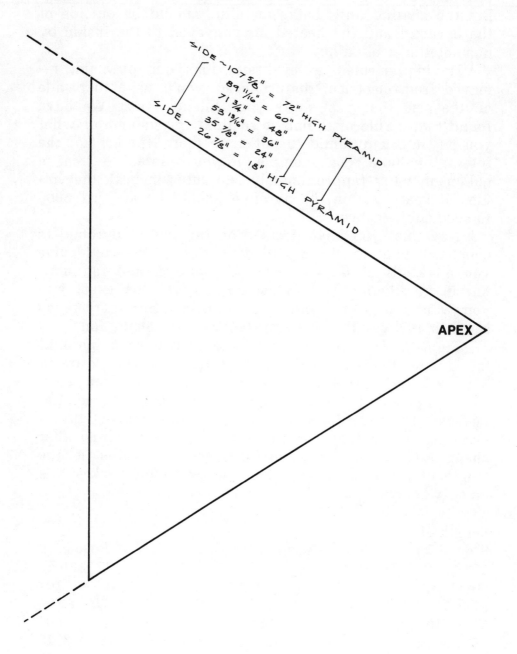

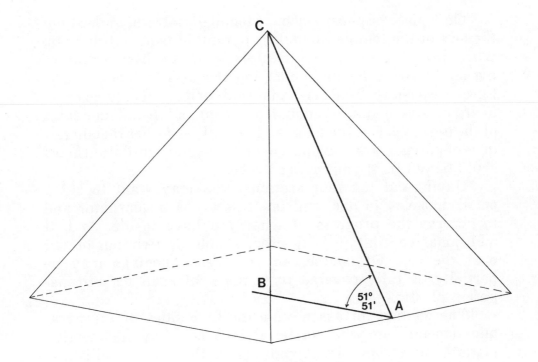

SLOPE ANGLE

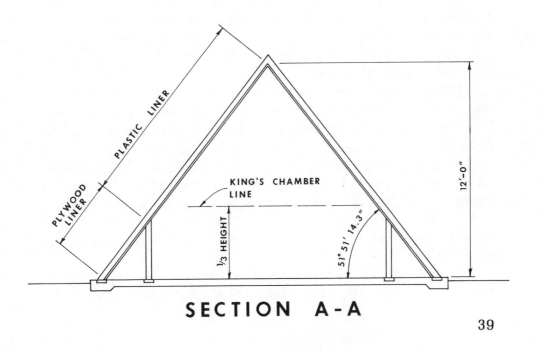

SECTION A-A

On a piece of paper trace the templet (pattern) and extend the legs of the templet to make a pyramid the height that you wish. (See table for length of legs for desired height of pyramid.) Draw a line connecting the legs to form a base. Purchase a sheet or sheets of material such as corrugated cardboard or plywood large enough to accommodate the four sides of the pyramid. Cut them out and join all four sides together. A door of polyglass or transparent material and ventilation holes could be put in at your convenience.

Having cut the four sections, you may want to cut a small doorway in one, and let it serve as a ventilator and to observe the progress of what you have inside. And, if additional ventilation is desired, a hole or two can be cut near the top. Of course, any of these openings may be partially or fully covered by a material such as a transparent plastic.

The method for assembling the four sides of the pyramid depends on what material is used. Any nonmetallic material is acceptable. Aluminum is the one metallic exception, provided it has been energized as explained in another section.

We strongly suggest that the beginning pyramid builder use corrugated paper board for his/her first project. Almost every city has a corrugated box factory that can supply sheets of material. It's easy to draw lines on and is economical to buy.

Glass tape is an amazingly strong and flexible material. It is excellent for joining the pyramid segments, and if a small amount of clearance is left between them, the finished pyramid can be folded flat for storage.

Normally a structure of this size need not have a base as it can be placed directly on the ground or floor of a room or building such as a garage or carport. But remember, it must be level. We find that using tapered wood shingles such as those used on roofs works quite well as leveling wedges.

You have already established a line to true north. Now, one side of your four-sided pyramid should be placed over this line and you're about ready to go. (See drawings.)

In an earlier section we stressed the importance of the King's Chamber area. In the case of a 3-foot pyramid, a shelf or table should be incorporated 1 foot from the surface the pyramid stands on, and the material to be treated placed on this surface.

Of course, a 3-foot plywood pyramid is only one example of the many variations that can be made. You may want to make a small model, perhaps out of cardboard, to keep in the bathroom for sharpening razor blades, or a much larger outdoor type such as we use for treatment of materials in volume. Or, you may want to extend the slope lines with wood, plastic, or aluminum "legs" and then cover the area with a flexible transparent plastic, or any textile material for a greenhouse effect.

But a word of warning. When a pyramid greenhouse is covered with a transparent material such as glass or clear plastic, heat may build up rapidly due to sun ray concentration, in spite of good ventilation. To guard against this it's wise to keep a supply of white cheese-cloth on hand to put over the pyramid during periods of extreme heat.

One further suggestion: If you have any trouble obtaining supplies, there is a reliable firm, Paragon Pyramid Products, Tucson, Arizona, that stocks finished pyramids in various sizes, components and materials for those people who want to build their own and other pyramid-related supplies. Paragon Pyramid Products also stocks the chemicals used in the personal care and gardening formulas in this book and will sell them by mail in quantities as small as one ounce. For further information on obtaining the materials called for in this book, write to:

Paragon Pyramid Products
P.O. Box 27163
Tucson, Arizona 85726

4

Pyramids for Meditation

The pyramid seems to enhance meditation for many people including myself. But before going into the procedures, it seems logical to understand the brain function that makes meditation and its benefits possible.

THE HUMAN BRAIN

Your own personal servant, your subconscious mind, is not a mythical thing, but rather a very real mass of cells, tissue, and miles of electrical circuits. The brain surgeon knows where it is, can see it and touch it, but doesn't himself know exactly how it works. To help your understanding as to why and how it can work for you, some of the functions of the brain are included here.

The human brain and nervous system are so complex that even scientists who have devoted a lifetime of study to them freely admit that there are many things about them which they do not know. It is known, however, that there are three basic portions of the brain that to a large degree control all of life's functions. In this control center electrical impulses are generated and transmitted to various parts of the body via the nervous system.

This system works conversely as well, for example, when you experience pain such as from a burn. Here the impulses are carried to the brain rather than from it. The nervous system has been likened to a vast telephone network that carries impulses, i.e., on and off bursts of electricity rather than a steady current. The speed of these impulses varies in accordance with the thickness of the nerve carrying them. Speeds range from a fraction of a millimeter in the smallest nerve fiber to 120 meters per second in the largest. If a person six feet tall were to stub his toe, the impulses would travel from the toe to the brain and back to the toe in less than 1/20th of a second.

Some impulses are voluntary and others involuntary. If you inadvertently touch a hot stove, you don't have to consciously think about removing your hand from the hot

Eileen Stark at Alpha level in the pyramid. Note Alpha wave electronic sensor.

surface. Or, if some object is coming toward your face, such as a ball, you don't think about raising your arm to shield it. These are involuntary reactions.

On the other hand, if you are sitting at a table and decide to pick up an object, you make the decision to reach for it. Or, if you decide to call someone on the telephone, it is your decision to dial the number. And in so doing you are programming your built-in guidance system to set the necessary machinery in motion to guide your hand to the object or your finger to the dial on the telephone.

When this happens an amazing set of circumstances takes place. Your desire to pick up the object or dial the number is transmitted to the subconscious control center by your conscious mind. Then your built-in goal-seeking mechanism takes over. Even if you were a specialist in anatomy, you couldn't direct the various muscles and nerves to react to each other to reach the goal. A very important point to remember is that consciously you have nothing to do with picking up the object or dialing the number other than to have the desire to do so.

Of the many functions of the brain, we are concerned with only two, the subconscious and the conscious. For the purpose of comparison, the subconscious is parallel to the electronic computer, and the conscious to the person who is programming (instructing) the computer as to what problem to work on.

THE SUBCONSCIOUS

As compared to computer technology, the subconscious mind works in two distinct but somewhat different ways, (1) as a problem-solving system where the answer to the problem is not known, and (2) as a guidance mechanism where the goal has been established. While some factors such as "memory storage" are common to both, the two functions are distinctly different. Almost everyone has had the experience of using his subconscious mind in some way but perhaps not realizing it. For example, you may have tried to recall a name and were unable to do so, and then a short time later it came to you. By trying to recall that name, you were instructing your subconscious to do it for you. It, in turn, scanned all the information stored in its memory system and flashed the answer back to your conscious mind. These are examples of how the team of the conscious and subconscious portions of your mind work to solve a known problem.

The second way in which the subconscious works is the one of primary concern. This mode of action can be compared to the electronic guidance system which controls the intercept missiles used in the nation's defense.

Our country is protected by a ring of interceptor missiles whose function, as the name implies, is to inter-

47

cept and destroy enemy projectiles should they ever be launched against us. To seek out and destroy an enemy missile requires a highly complex electronic guidance system to guide our defense projectile to its target. Factors which must be taken into account to predetermine that the two will meet at the desired location are the interception point, speed of the missile, trajectory, direction, windage, initial velocity, and the rate at which the velocity decreases. To make it possible for our defensive missile to meet its target its electronic guidance system must be equipped with sensing devices such as radar, etc., to accomplish its goal. Remember, the goal (enemy missile), must be known just as you know what your goal is.

To travel to its target the guidance system utilizes the principle of feedback, which, simply put, is nothing more than the continuous correction of errors. Perhaps one of the simplest examples of feedback is the temperature control in the oven of your electric or gas range. Suppose you are preparing a roast that you desire to cook at a temperature of 350° F. You set your control for that temperature, but the thermostat does not hold the temperature precisely at that point. When you turn on the electricity or gas to the oven, the temperature begins to rise. When it reaches 350° F., the setting you want, the power does not turn off. Rather, it goes beyond the selected temperature by several degrees, at which time the thermostat recognizes that it has made a mistake and corrects it by turning off the power. Now, when the temperature falls below the selected setting, it again senses its error and turns the heat back on.

Electronic and mechanical guidance systems are fantastic to be sure. But let's take a look at what our own built-in guidance system (subconscious mind) can do if we wish to see something infinitely more fantastic.

Let's assume that you enjoy the game of tennis. Your racket has a hitting area of only about a square foot, and the ball you are going to hit is only 2-1/2 to 3 inches in diameter. Your opponent serves the ball over the net to you, and your goal is to intercept it with your racket (just as the interceptor missile contacts the invading missile) and hit it back to your opponent. To hit the ball your guidance system must *automatically* and at lightning speed take into account the speed of the ball, wind direction and velocity, degree of drop, the point where the ball hits the court and direction of the bounce.

To hit the ball with the strings of the racket, your guidance system must make the necessary calculations at speeds in fractions of seconds. You don't even think about this. Your built-in guidance system takes care of it for you automatically. It receives the necessary data via your eyes and ears, from which it triggers muscle and nerve reactions automatically to guide the racket to its goal, the ball. Fantastic? It certainly is.

Still another parallel between the electronic and the human guidance systems can be illustrated in the operation of an automobile. We discussed feedback in conjunction with the missile and the temperature control. The subconscious guidance system operates in the same way. When you drive your car down the road, you establish your desired path of travel. However, even the most experienced test driver is unable to follow the exact path. When the car wanders to one side of it, the subconscious signals that an error has been made, and a correction is effected by your muscles adjusting the steering wheel. And again when it crosses the line of desired travel in the opposite direction, a mistake is signaled and a correction made. And all of this is done without conscious effort. The eyes set up the desire or goal, and the subconscious guidance system does the rest automatically through your nerve and muscle systems.

DEFINITION AND FUNCTIONS

The subconscious mind, as has previously been described, is and can be used as an automatic mechanism that seeks the best possible method to achieve the goal we set for it to accomplish.

Like the electronic computer, it records, classifies, and stores all the information that has ever been fed to it by the senses, i.e., sight, sound, touch, and smell, and keeps them ready for use at any time. The subconscious works at all times, whether we are asleep or awake. A number of leading universities have conducted extensive studies which prove beyond question it is possible to learn in your sleep. Tape recordings have been played to subjects while in deep sleep, and it was found that the material could be recalled by the conscious mind when the subject awoke.

Unlike the conscious mind through which we have been taught the difference between right and wrong as children, the subconscious does not know this difference. A racketeer or criminal who knows how to use it can put the subconscious to work for his benefit just as a great scientist or physician, working for the benefit of man, can put his subconscious to work for good. Just as a gun can be put to use for obtaining food, or can be used for evil such as robbery, the subconscious guidance mechanism can be put to any use for which it is instructed (programmed).

While the subconscious, as we have seen, can be controlled to suit our desires, it performs many fantastic functions that we do not consciously control. Among just a few of these are: breathing, heartbeat, blood pressure, and involuntary muscle reactions such as blinking of eyelids. And, as a chemical manufacturing plant, it makes our giant chemical factories look like a child's chemistry set.

We have all read of cases (and perhaps some of us have experienced them) where people have performed what appeared to be superhuman feats of strength or courage in an emergency situation. This is made possible by the sudden spurt in the production of adrenalin. This chemical is secreted by the adrenal glands in normal amounts to fill the bodily needs. When fear, anger, or danger are present, however, the glands are stimulated and super amounts are produced and injected into the bloodstream. This stimulates the sympathetic nervous system, causing an increase in blood pressure, respiration, and muscular exertions. This is just one example of the almost unbelievable way the human brain fills the body's own needs *automatically*.

The subconscious and all that it controls is set into motion (programmed) by the thoughts fed to it by the conscious mind. The mother *sees* a heavy object fall on her child. She *knows* she must lift it off. These senses trigger her subconscious mind, which immediately produces adrenalin, giving her the strength she must have to lift the heavy weight from her child. A demand made on the subconscious is most effective when liberally mixed with emotion. Again in the case of the mother and child she *sees* the trouble, *hears* the cries, and *knows* she must do something. But, in addition, she is terrified for the child's safety which adds the emotion of *fear*. The subconscious best understands the language of emotion, but the demand must be clear cut and not wishy-washy. The mother knew she *must* help her child, no question about it, and this enabled her to do it.

HOW TO PROGRAM
THE SUBCONSCIOUS IN THE PYRAMID

Throughout this chapter the similarity between the electronic computer and the subconscious mind has been explained and is continued in this section on programming.

A computer costing hundreds of thousands of dollars is really nothing more than a complex arrangement of parts that are of little value to anyone unless they are put to work. And to make them work they must be instructed (programmed) by a human as to what problem to work on or what function to guide, just as our human control center must be.

When a child is told to pick up his shoes and put them in a closet, he does it because he has learned by previous training how to do so and he understands the instructions. Or when he is assigned an arithmetic problem to do, he understands the assignment, and is able to complete it because he has learned numbers and their values. Likewise the computer must be instructed in language that it "understands."

As we know, the computer is a dormant machine until someone applies electrical power to it and tells it what to do. Not so in the case of the subconscious mind. The subconscious mind in all of us started functioning the day we were born and continues till the day we die. It can't be turned on or off as a computer can. Therefore, it is *always* subject to being programmed by thoughts fed to it by the senses through the conscious mind.

Herein lies a real danger that must be guarded against. Since the subconscious works for good or bad and doesn't know the difference, it can be programmed for an undesirable as well as for a desirable effect. Here's a good example of how this works.

This story has been told about one of the greatest woman tennis players of all time. She was playing a very close match with a formidable opponent and holding her own very well. During the break her coach warned her *not* to make a certain serve to her opponent. You guessed it. She did, and lost the game. What happened was that the coach's negative thought was transmitted through her conscious mind to her subconscious where it was acted upon, causing the wrong serve to be offered.

The most effective way to program the subconscious is by autosuggestion, and the most effective method of producing autosuggestion is by the combination of *sight* and *sound*. One of the best examples of this is the television commercial—the purpose of which is to induce you to buy the product being advertised.

Seeing and hearing simultaneously is far more effective than seeing or hearing independently. Let's assume an advertisement for a cosmetic product comes to you via radio and has a receptive value of 10. Assume further now that a magazine ad containing the identical copy also has a value of 10. That same ad on T.V. will have a reception value of many times the total of 20, because the impact on the subconscious mind is far greater in combination with sight and sound than with sight or sound independently.

But sight and sound alone are not sufficient to reliably set your subconscious mind to work. Before it will accept a job and do it, the element of *vivid desire* must be conveyed. A halfhearted wish won't do. And, this must be conveyed in the form of a forceful demand. A firmly held purpose or desire must be coupled with faith and belief that it will be fulfilled. This belief must be so strong that it becomes a foregone conclusion that the subconscious will carry out the demands fed to it. The computer operator *knows* that when he programs the machine he *will* get a result. He knows this because he has had repeated experiences where his machine has performed for him. Likewise you *know* your subconscious mind will carry out your demands when properly instructed because it has done so for you before. Scores of people attest to the fact that it works, including many leaders in the field of medicine and science. You yourself have had experiences (such as recalling a name) that prove that it works. By an inexplicable law, what we expect and believe comes to us. This works, make no mistake about it.

Impulses of thought, when properly programmed, bring about their physical equivalent by setting the subconscious to work to manifest them.

One of the ways in which the electronic computer does differ from the subconscious, however, is that it does not have competition for its attention. Unless the operator is programming, it is a dormant machine. When receiving instructions it is not subjected to counterinstructions. Conversely, the subconscious is constantly being bombarded with sights and sounds that the conscious mind has not intentionally programmed.

It has been established that positive thoughts, properly programmed, replace negative ones. This is true, however, *only* if the positive thought is repeated with persistence over and over. Therefore, it is essential that the thought you want your subconscious to work on leaves no room for its counterpart. This is accomplished by persistently holding to the positive thought by frequent repetition.

The subconscious can easily be deceived and fooled, wherein lies one of the great secrets of using it successfully to accomplish a goal. It accepts as fact anything that is impressed upon it often enough and convincingly enough, and proceeds to make it come true. Therefore, when you "sell" it on the idea that the circumstance you desire *already exists*, it proceeds to cause it to exist. When a seed is planted in the ground, it attracts to it the air, water, and food necessary for its growth. Likewise, a desire (seed) purposefully held in the mind causes the subconscious to create its physical equivalent. Transcendental meditation (TM) has moved from the occult to scientific acceptance in recent years. It has now been given the recognition of a valid science and is practiced by thousands of people all over the world. Well-respected publications, including technical journals such as *Chemical Engineering News,* have carried articles about it, and some universities are now starting to teach it. The key to TM is *relaxation,* and this is where a pyramid becomes an invaluable tool.

There are four basic levels of brain activity that emit electrical waves at different frequencies. They are: Beta (about 14 to 28 cycles per second), Alpha (8 to 13 cycles per second), Theta (4 to 7 cycles per second), and Delta (1/2 to 4 cycles per second). Of these the primary objective in TM is to reach the Alpha level. At this level the brain emits a wave pattern that is conducive to relaxation, tranquility, creativity, and a general sense of well-being. And, while this level can be reached without the aid of a pyramid, as can be attested to by many people who practice it regularly, it is much easier to accomplish inside a pyramid, and seems to me to be a more complete transition to the Alpha level.

Although I have made an in-depth study of mind control over the years, even before it was widely accepted, and use it constantly in my life and in my work, I feel the science should be taught on a person-to-person basis. There are many qualified professional instructors available for this purpose. However, I do want to share my procedures and methods in the hope that readers will benefit from them.

It has been found that the best location in the pyramid for meditation is at the location of the King's Chamber, below the apex. The meditator may assume either a lying down or a sitting position. In either case—the body should be aligned to the true north line which would, of course, be parallel to the side of the pyramid that's on the north/south line. Clothing should be loose and comfortable.

When an electronic computer is to be programmed, the first thing the programmer does is to clear it of any previous information it may have in the storage system. If this were not done, data retained in the memory bank would affect the new program. And the same thing applies to the human mind. Before a subject can be dealt with successfully all previous thoughts must be erased. Here's one method that works, at least for me, inside the pyramid.

The Alpha level of mind (subconscious) is below the Beta (conscious) level of mind as demonstrated by the fact that Beta emits electrical impulses in the range of 14 to 28 cycles per second, while Alpha is in the lower range of 8 to 13. Therefore, I feel it necessary to go down to reach this level. Many TM instructors teach various ways to reach Alpha. All are good, but many people find some methods better than others. The one I use that works well for me is less complex than some of the others, but embodies basic principles of "going down to Alpha" in the pyramid. Here are the procedures.

1. Before entering the pyramid the goal to be attained should be clearly established. But, remember the goal must be singular. If it isn't, it can't work. Here is an example. If your goal was stated as having a lot of money, good health, and a rapport with family and friends, your subconscious mind would be so confused that nothing would work. So, if these three things are your goals, they must be handled individually.

You must be specific. If you need money, exactly how much? If it's health, specify what you want to heal. If it's rapport with people, who's the person? A son or daughter possibly? But narrow it down to one problem, and then concentrate on it to the exclusion of all else.

2. Having established the goal that you are going to work on when you get to Alpha in the pyramid, you're ready to start.

3. Either sit or lie down in a comfortable position at King's Chamber height. Loosen all clothing such as belts, shoelaces, etc. Your position should be parallel to either the east or west side of the pyramid, which will align your body to true north. Close your eyes and relax your body. You'll find this much easier to do in the pyramid than outside of it.

4. We know that brain waves of Alpha (8 to 13 cycles per second) are below those of Beta (14 to 28 cycles per second). Therefore, I like to think of going "down" to Alpha.

5. I imagine myself in an elevator with #10 assigned to the level at the start of descent. Then, as I mentally push the button that equals #0, the elevator starts to descend until it stops at #0, and the doors open.

6. At this point the subject should be looking at a scene that is peaceful and quiet. Perhaps a memory from

childhood as mine is. I see a pastoral panorama consisting of a green meadow with a trout brook tumbling through it, and cattle grazing peacefully on a warm summer day. Actually, this is a scene I have been exposed to many times as a boy on my grandmother's farm in Wisconsin.

7. Let's assume that the purpose of going to Alpha is to help a family member suffering from crippling arthritis of the hands. Imagine that a harsh-colored disc of light appears, and centered in it the image of gnarled, deformed hands can be seen. Now a second disc of a soft pastel color appears and slowly passes over the first disc, obliterating the image of the sick hands, much in the way an eclipse of the moon appears. And inside the pastel disc is the image of healthy, normal hands.

We know that the subconscious mind, like its counterpart the electronic computer, can act on only one thing at a time. And by erasing the first negative picture, the subconscious is freed to act on the positive image and bring it to fruition.

8. Now the sun is beginning to set, old Shep has rounded up the cattle and taken them to the barn for milking, so it's time to return up to the Beta level. To do this, I get into my imaginary elevator, set the button to #10 and slowly ascend, opening the eyes when the elevator stops and the doors open.

This is but one way to utilize Alpha. There are many others. The interested reader will find many good books on the subject as well as private instruction and continuing adult education courses offered by many colleges and universities. As previously stated this section is not intended to teach TM, but rather to explain how the pyramid can aid in achieving total relaxation which is essential to successful meditation.

5

Pyramids for Energizing
Water and Aluminum

ENERGIZED WATER

As we explained in a previous section, the energy found in the pyramid can be transferred simply by storing water in the pyramid at the King's Chamber level.

It is important to remember that your pyramid should be of sufficient size so that what is put into it does not exceed about 5 percent of its volume. We store our water in five-gallon plastic containers at King's Chamber height and transfer it to smaller plastic containers as it is needed. In this way we always have a supply being energized. A rule of thumb is that twenty-four hours is adequate time for one gallon. This may vary depending upon geographic location. However, it is simple to determine when the water is ready by holding your needle over the top of the container outside of the pyramid. If it oscil-

Energizing water in the pyramid.

lates, the energy transfer has been made. If not, more time in the pyramid is needed.

There are many uses for energized water where it excels over plain tap water. When pyramid water is used on house plants, the growth rate is substantially increased and the color of leaves and flowers intensified greatly.

The ladies swear that using energized water as a face wash has a beneficial effect on the complexion, and as a hair rinse, it brings out the highlights.

We use pyramid water for drinking, and feel that the taste is better than ordinary untreated water. This applies to making coffee, tea, and all sorts of drinks as well.

Our research garden is planted with seeds that are germinated in the pyramid greenhouse using energized water. Seedlings are also treated in the pyramid before planting. Careful testing has demonstrated beyond a doubt that these seeds and seedlings grow to maturity in up to 2/3 the time required by those planted in the conventional way.

ENERGIZED ALUMINUM

Another strange phenomenon of the pyramid mystery is that aluminum has the property of being able to store pyramid energy and then release it when it has become saturated. It then literally becomes a generator making it possible, as with water, to transport energy out of the pyramid to remote locations.

The aluminum to be energized can be either in the form of bars, solid sheets, or flexible foil. Regardless of which is used, however, it should be aligned to the true north/south line which would be achieved by placing it parallel to either the east or west side at the King's Chamber level.

Generally it takes a longer time for aluminum to adsorb the energy than it does for water to do so. We find that a good policy is to permit the roll of foil or sheets to

Both left and right cuttings started on same date. Left cutting in pyramid water with energized aluminum foil around glass. Right cutting in non-pyramid water without foil.

remain in the pyramid for about two weeks, and then when not in use, store them on the King's Chamber shelf. The same needle test used on water to determine when it is charged may be used on aluminum as well.

1. Use the foil, cut in circles, under potted plants to speed growth and produce a healthier plant.

2. Wrap foil around the glass that cuttings are being started in.

3. Wrap foil around meat to be roasted. Cooking time will be cut dramatically.

4. Wrap energized foil around pipe tobacco, cigars, or cigarettes for a much smoother smoke.

5. Before brewing wrap ground coffee or tea in energized foil for about 10 minutes. You'll be surprised at how much better your coffee or tea will taste.

6. And, while this subject is controversial, some peo-

ple claim that wrapping energized foil around areas of pain, such as joints, brings relief. While we obviously can't prescribe this use, we do think it's worth a try for the many folks who suffer from pain caused by arthritis and other illnesses.

6

Pyramids for Health
and Beauty

CAUTION TO READERS

All chemicals that are stored in containers should be labeled, regardless of whether they are a raw material or a finished compound. This is basic, and must be followed in the interest of safety. Keep all chemicals out of the reach of children, and note the contents on the label. In this way if a child, or even an unsuspecting adult, should accidentally consume the contents, the doctor would know what treatment to initiate. While these formulas have been chosen with an eye to safety, many materials normally regarded as safe can be dangerous if taken internally, or to excess.

In those formulas in which it is felt that there is a possibility of allergic reaction, it is suggested that the formulas be applied to a small test area to determine if an allergic reaction takes place and if it does, use should be discontinued. However, if the reader or user of the formulas is prone to allergic reaction, all personal products should be tested in this way.

If the material is toxic by inhalation, use with adequate ventilation. If it is harmful by ingestion, call a physician or poison control center immediately if it has been ingested. If it is an irritant to skin, flush freely with water. If flammable, as are waxes and oils as well as other materials such as solvents, keep the chemical away from open flame or excessive heat.

Although high precision is not required, measurements should be accurate. Standard U.S. measuring spoons and measuring cups should be used. Teaspoons and tablespoons are level spoonfuls. The same is true for cups, half cups, and so on.

Here's an example of a safe label.

```
This Bottle Contains _____
Its Ingredient(s) are:



Keep out of reach of children.

Made by _____

Date _____
                KEEP BOTTLE SEALED
```

HOW THE PYRAMID MAY HELP HEALTH

Most physicians whose opinions I have read or whom I have queried personally seem to agree that while tension is frequently associated with poor health, relaxation is often associated with good health. And we do know from many tests that the pyramid is conducive to relaxation in the great majority of people exposed to its energy. I hasten to make it known that I am not a medical doctor. Therefore, I can only report experiences in health improvement that I have been told of or have witnessed.

Arizona, because of its dryness, is a mecca for folks suffering from arthritis. And, I understand that some are helped while other types are not. It's a sad sight indeed to see people with deformed bodies, suffering constant pain. We have seen repeated instances in which some people claim to have had relief after exposure to pyramid energy. Since this is such a simple, inexpensive procedure, it seems to make sense for a person suffering from arthritis to try it and see if it helps.

While the good Lord has seen fit to spare me from arthritis, I do have a chronic blood disorder that requires periodic blood counts. On one occasion, during a period when I was not under treatment, a strange thing occurred. There was a radical change in my blood picture which my hematologist was unable to explain. And just before the count I had been spending a great deal of time in the pyramid.

This doctor is associated with a leading medical research team, and his interest was aroused to the extent that he suggested a blood study on a colony of laboratory mice to determine if the accidental discovery could be verified. We intend to start this program soon, and will have reportable data for the next book in this series on pyramids. Whether it turns out to be a valid theory or not, I feel so much better that I wouldn't think of stopping my daily exposure to pyramid energy.

High blood pressure (hypertension) is a killer disease

that affects up to 15 percent of the adult population of the United States. Because there are often no symptoms in the earlier stages, it is frequently not detected until it progresses to a more advanced degree. Not withstanding the other important advantages, this in itself makes periodic medical checkups very important.

According to the medical literature (e.g., *The Merck Manual,* Twelfth Edition) there are many different causes for high blood pressure that the physician knows how to treat with medications available to him. But one of the leading causes, perhaps in combination with other factors, is tension—the opposite of relaxation.

A certain amount of tension is said to be normal in most people. The word "hyper" means excessive. Therefore, the word hypertension (synonymous with high blood pressure) means excessive tension.

We know from experience that exposure to pyramid energy is highly conducive to relaxation. With rare exceptions, people who spend time in a pyramid report a feeling of tranquility and relaxation.

Because of obvious correlations between tension and elevated blood pressure, we believe that reducing tension and increasing relaxation by pyramid energy may have a lowering effect on blood pressure. A number of indications have strongly suggested this possibility. However, a full-scale testing program is necessary to either confirm or deny it.

To this end, we have talked with a number of physicians who are willing to ask some of their hypertensive patients to participate in the study, the results of which should be available in the next book in the pyramid series.

It is suggested that readers with a high blood pressure problem may want to experiment on their own, with the specific approval of a medical doctor, of course. Any results obtained would be gratefully received, and will be incorporated into our overall study.

PYRAMID WATER USED IN BEAUTY
AND PERSONAL CARE FORMULAS

As we have seen in previous sections of this book, water exposed to pyramid energy undergoes remarkable changes in chemical makeup. One of the most interesting is the nitrogen content of the water.

A number of people who have used energized pyramid water as a face wash and final hair rinse claim complexion and hair sheen improvement. We are at a loss to explain this; however, nitrogen is essential to a plant's growth and healthy appearance, so perhaps it also has a beneficial effect on human cells.

Following are some easy to make formulas, using pyramid water, for the readers who may want to experiment with them. But husbands—if your wife suddenly looks twenty-five again, and runs off with a college football hero, don't come after me with your shotgun. We're only suggesting.

In those formulas in which it is felt that there is a possibility of allergic reaction, it is suggested that the formulas be applied to a small test area to determine if an allergic reaction takes place and if it does, use should be discontinued. However, if the reader or user of the formulas is prone to allergic reactions, all personal products should be tested in this way.

It is also suggested that all containers and mixing utensils for personal care formulas, especially those used near the eyes, should be sterilized or at least thoroughly washed.

Some of these personal care formulas call for the use of alcohol.

There are two types of alcohol that can be used for making these formulas, (1) isopropyl, or (2) denatured. Denatured alcohol is ethyl alcohol that has been intentionally adulterated to make it unfit for human consumption. Many different chemicals are used as additives depending on the end use of the alcohol. For example, alcohol that is to be used as an industrial solvent would be far more drastically denatured than alcohol that is to be used as a rubbing compound. But remember, all denatured alcohols must not be taken internally as they are toxic to varying degrees. They are also flammable, of course.

Isopropyl alcohol is my choice for a number of reasons. (1) It is readily available in small quantities; (2) it is lower in cost; and (3) although it is toxic it is far less so than most of the denatured alcohols. But it is also flammable and should be used with the proper precautions.

ASTRINGENT SKIN LOTION

Ingredients:

Pyramid water	3 cups
Glycerin	1 tablespoon
Powdered alum	2 tablespoons
Water soluble perfume	to suit

To ease the sting and stop the bleeding from scratches, shaving nicks, and small cuts, mix 1 tablespoon glycerin into 3 cups water, and stir in 2 tablespoons of powdered alum. Store in bottles and apply with cotton on face or neck before bedtime. Glycerin and alum may be obtained at a drugstore.

ASTRINGENT SKIN CREAM

Ingredients:

Pyramid water	1 cup
Mineral oil	2 cups
White beeswax	1/2 cup
Powdered borax	1-1/2 tablespoons
Powdered alum	2 tablespoons

While this formula is not really difficult to make, it is

somewhat more complex than others. As we all know, oil and water will not mix. So to combine them we need to form an emulsion, that is to disperse the oil droplets throughout the mixture so they are held in suspension.

An astringent is a material that contracts the tissues of the skin causing a tightening effect. In this formula, powdered alum is the ingredient that accomplishes this function.

Heat the mineral oil and beeswax together in the top of a double boiler (never over an open flame) until the beeswax is melted and mixed with the mineral oil. Cool down to 120 degrees F. Now in a separate pan, heat the pyramid water to 120 degrees and stir in the borax and alum, mixing until dissolved. Next, pour the mixture of borax, alum and water slowly into the mixture of mineral oil and beeswax with constant stirring. When the final mixture has cooled down to just above the solidification point, a few drops of oil-soluble perfume may be added as desired. Store in glass or plastic jars. Mineral oil and alum may be obtained from a drugstore or chemical supply house, white beeswax from a hobby shop, and borax at a grocery store or hardware store. Mineral oil is flammable.

Use this cream to smooth and firm skin on face and neck and around elbows and ankles.

(Caution: Undiluted powdered borax is toxic by ingestion. If, when used regularly, it causes a rash discontinue use.)

LIME AND GLYCERIN CREAM

Ingredients:

Almond extract	1/8 teaspoon
Glycerin	1/8 teaspoon
Lemon extract	1/8 teaspoon
Lime	1
Pyramid water	1 cup

A pleasant and soothing cream may be made with

lime water. Soak several slices of a whole lime in pyramid water overnight, then to the 1 cup of lime water, add 1/8 teaspoon of glycerin, 1/8 teaspoon lemon extract and stir in 1/8 teaspoon of almond extract. Stir thoroughly and bottle in glass or plastic containers. Apply to skin as desired.

All ingredients in this formula may be obtained at a drugstore.

TOILETTE WATER

Ingredients:

Isopropyl alcohol	5 tablespoons
Glycerin	5 tablespoons
Borax	2 tablespoons
Pyramid water	1 quart
Water soluble perfume	to suit

Perfume goes back for centuries and has been widely used since then. While there are many kinds of perfumes, including synthetics made in the laboratory, the most common are those derived from plants. In some plants, the fragrant oils, known as essential oil, are present in the leaves while in others they are present in the flowers.

The essential oils are extracted by means of steam distillation whereby the flowers or leaves are boiled with water and the steam is condensed back into liquid form. This condensate is then redistilled to separate the oil and water; however, some of the oil does remain with the water, which then becomes known as rose water, lavender water, etc. These are the fragrances called for in this formula.

Mix all the ingredients together, stirring as each one is put in. Store in capped glass or impervious plastic containers. (Caution: Isopropyl alcohol is flammable and toxic. Undiluted borax is toxic by ingestion. If, when used regularly, it causes a rash discontinue use.) Isopropyl alcohol and glycerin may be obtained from a drugstore or chemical supply house, and borax from a hardware or grocery store.

FACIAL PORE CLOSER

Ingredients:

Powdered alum	1 tablespoon
Talc	1 cup
Boric acid	1 tablespoon
Isopropyl alcohol	1/2 cup
Pyramid water	1 cup

Skin performs many functions for us. It acts as a waterproof covering for the body, transmits signals to the brain, excretes wastes, and aids in the control of body temperature. Where I live, in toasty Tucson, the humidity is low and 100 degrees plus temperatures are common in summer months. Getting out of a swimming pool is quite an experience in that your skin becomes ice cold. This is caused by the rapid evaporation of water on the skin, and works on the same principle as a mechanical refrigeration unit.

The skin contains sebaceous glands that secrete the oil which collects in the pores. Now add dust and dirt, which we are all exposed to, and the plugged pores result in blackheads and skin infections. But these problems can be reduced by treating the pores with an astringent to reduce the possibility of their being collectors of dirt. Here's the way to do it.

All containers and mixing utensils should be sterilized or at least completely washed. Mix the isopropyl alcohol with the pyramid water, and add the alum, talc and boric acid to the solution. To use, wash face thoroughly to remove accumulated dirt and oil. Before bedtime apply facial pore closer liberally with cotton. Rinse with clear water in the morning. Store in glass or plastic containers.

(Caution: Isopropyl alcohol is toxic and flammable. Undiluted boric acid is toxic by ingestion. If, when used regularly, it causes a rash discontinue use.)

Isopropyl alcohol may be obtained from a drugstore or solvent distributor. The remaining ingredients may be purchased from a drugstore or chemical supply house.

WINTER HAND PROTECTIVE LOTION

Ingredients:

Unflavored gelatin	1 envelope
Glycerin	3/4 cup
Pyramid water	1-1/2 cups

When the skin on your hands looks like ice skaters' tracks on a pond and when they feel like the blades of the ice skates have been cutting into them, a store-bought lotion may leave you smelling like flowers—but no better protected than if you make your own.

Make up this simple mixture to use *before* exposure to the elements for real protection. Rub it on your hands again after you've worked outside for added effectiveness.

Heat one envelope of gelatin (the unflavored kind from the grocery store) and 3/4 cup glycerin in the top of a double boiler. Add 1-1/2 cups of pyramid water slowly, pouring in a constant stream while stirring the mixture. Water-soluble perfume may be added if desired. Apply sparingly to skin before exposure to winter weather.

Glycerin may be obtained at a drugstore.

FINGERNAIL HARDENER

Ingredients:

Powdered alum	1 teaspoon
Glycerin	1 tablespoon
Pyramid water	3 tablespoons

In the midst of her whirlwind activities, today's woman may want to feel and look more attractive, and this desire includes well-groomed fingernails. As her hands are ever moving, her fingernails are constantly being abused and often broken. Not every woman has the time or the money to spend for frequent manicures, and an economical way for her to keep nails attractive and healthy is to use the following easily prepared formula.

Mix 1 tablespoon of glycerin with 3 tablespoons of pyramid water. Then add 1 teaspoon of powdered alum and stir until dissolved. Both the glycerin and alum are available at any drugstore. To use, coat the fingernails with this solution at night before bedtime and remove in the morning with isopropyl alcohol. Continue use each night until the desired degree of hardness is attained.

(Caution: Isopropyl alcohol is toxic and flammable.)

FINGERNAIL SOFTENER

Ingredients:

Triethanolamine, technical or manufacturing grade, not U.S.P.	3 tablespoons
Olive oil	2 tablespoons
Pyramid water	1/2 cup

If on the other hand, your nails are so hard and dry that they crack and chip and you want to soften them up, paint them with a mixture of 3 tablespoons triethanolamine in 1/2 cup pyramid water, to which you slowly stir in 2 tablespoons of olive oil. This can be washed off in the morning.

Note: U.S.P. grade triethanolamine is under prescription in some states. The technical or manufacturing grade may be obtained from a drugstore or chemical supply house. Olive oil may be purchased at any grocery store. (Caution: triethanolamine may be somewhat irritating to skin and mucous membranes.)

LEMON HAIR RINSE

Ingredients:
Lemon extract   20 drops
Pyramid water   2 cups

Mix the lemon extract with the pyramid water and store in glass or plastic containers. Use as a final hair rinse after shampooing. Lemon extract may be obtained at a drugstore or grocery store.

LATHER OR ELECTRIC PRESHAVE LOTION

Ingredients:
Silicone oil emulsion   2 tablespoons
Pyramid water   2 cups

For a preshave lotion to smooth your skin and stiffen your beard, mix 2 tablespoons of silicone oil emulsion with 2 cups pyramid water. Add a few drops of a water base perfume if desired. Store in glass or plastic containers. For lather shaving, apply to skin while face is wet. For electric shaving, apply and allow skin to dry before shaving.

Silicone oil emulsion may be obtained from a chemical supply house or foundry supply.

AFTERSHAVE LOTION

Ingredients:
Pyramid water   2 cups
Isopropyl alcohol   1 cup
Glycerin   2 tablespoons
Boric acid   1 teaspoon

Using a soothing and refreshing lotion after shaving

is a pleasant experience for any man. But it's not so pleasant to buy it at about ten times what you can make it for.

Measure the pyramid water into a container. Add the isopropyl alcohol to the water. Next, add 2 tablespoons of glycerin and 1 teaspoon of boric acid. If you want to smell nice, add a few drops of your favorite cologne. (Caution: Isopropyl alcohol is toxic and flammable. Undiluted boric acid is toxic by ingestion. If, when used regularly, it causes a rash discontinue use.) Store in glass or plastic containers.

Isopropyl alcohol may be obtained from a druggist; boric acid and glycerin from a drugstore or chemical supply house.

LANOLIN HAND AND FACE LOTION

Ingredients:

Powdered soap	1/2 teaspoon
Pyramid water	2 tablespoons
Lanolin	2 tablespoons
Glycerin	2 tablespoons

By and large, the wool we use for clothing and other fabrics has the lanolin removed from it. There is a notable exception however. Our Canadian friends do not remove the lanolin from some wool that is used to knit the heavy sweaters so popular in that beautiful cold country. By leaving the fat in the wool, a high degree of water repellency results serving as protection against rain and snow. Here's a formula for a hand and face cream that contains lanolin as an important ingredient.

Mix the soap and glycerin into the pyramid water. Now add the lanolin with constant, rapid stirring. Water-soluble perfume may be added as desired. Use as you would any face or hand cream. Store in glass or plastic containers.

The ingredients may be obtained from a drugstore or chemical supply house.

SWEDISH MOUTHWASH

Ingredients:

Pyramid water	4 cups
Borax	1/16 teaspoon
Boric acid	1-1/2 teaspoons
Red food coloring	pinch
Oil of cloves	2 drops

From Sweden—the land of superb engineering, sensational movie actresses, a rather militant neutrality and one of the highest standards of living in the world—a mouthwash? Yes, and a good one, too. Here's how to make it.

Measure out the water and mix in the borax, boric acid and red food coloring. Now add a few drops of oil of cloves, or steep several cloves in the mixture and bottle in a glass or plastic container.

The boric acid and oil of cloves may be purchased at a drugstore; red food coloring and borax from a grocery store.

(Caution: Undiluted boric acid and borax are toxic by ingestion. If, when used regularly, it causes a rash, discontinue use.)

OXYGEN FOOT BATH

Ingredients:

Sodium thiosulfate	1 tablespoon
Sodium perborate	1 tablespoon
Sodium borate	6 tablespoons
Sodium bicarbonate	3/4 cup
Pyramid water	2 quarts for each foot bath

It has been said that bread is the staff of life. But

this is not entirely true. I vote for oxygen. Oxygen is absolutely essential to life.

Here's a formula that releases oxygen to soothe tired feet. Try it and I think you'll find it beneficial, as I have.

Dry-mix the above ingredients together, except for the pyramid water. Store in glass or plastic containers. To use, mix 2 tablespoons of mixture in 2 quarts of pyramid water for a foot bath. The released bubbling action makes for a soothing and relaxing experience.

Sodium thiosulfate may be obtained from a photographic supply store; the rest of the ingredients may be found at a drugstore or chemical supply house.

(Note: Sodium perborate and sodium borate are moderately toxic by ingestion.)

BEAUTY CLAY

Ingredients:

Powdered clay	2-1/2 pounds
Tincture of benzoin	1/8 cup
Pyramid water	to suit

Beauty clay is probably as old as cosmetics themselves. I've read somewhere that Cleopatra splashed river mud on her skin as a beauty aid. Whether it did any good or not is unknown. She did have a way with the boys, however. So who knows?

Many women travel to beauty spas where the mud is supposed to have skin-rejuvenating powers. Again, who knows? But it's my guess that any material such as mud or clay has a "drawing effect" when it dries, just like the poultice that grandma used to slap on our chest when we caught a bad cold.

So before you spend $20.00 or $30.00 for a beauty-clay facial at your local salon, why not try this formula for about 10¢ per treatment. But remember, if you land a job as a model or movie star, I'll expect a royalty.

All containers and mixing utensils for this formula should be sterilized or at least thoroughly washed. Mix the tincture of benzoin into the clay. (Note: A flour sifter is excellent for this and will also remove lumps and foreign matter.) Store mixture in a glass or plastic container. To use: Take about 1 cup of this mixture and add pyramid water slowly with constant stirring until a thick creamlike consistency results. Paint this mixture to about 1/8″ thickness on face with a soft brush. Allow to dry for about an hour and wash off with clear water.

Powdered clay may be purchased at a chemical supply house, building material dealer, or ceramic shop. Tincture of benzoin is not benzoin. It is most commonly called gum benzoin and is available from the drugstore.

BLONDE HAIR RINSE

Ingredients:

Pyramid water	3-3/4 cups
Tincture of rhubarb	2-1/2 tablespoons
Isopropyl alcohol	1/3 cup
Propylene glycol	2 teaspoons

To use as a rinse after shampooing on light-colored hair, this preparation will bring out those glowing highlights especially when pyramid water is used. Mix the pyramid water with the tincture of rhubarb, isopropyl alcohol, and propylene glycol. A few drops of your favorite oil-based perfume may be added if you wish. Store in airtight containers. The tincture of rhubarb and the isopropyl alcohol may be purchased at a drugstore; the propylene glycol from a chemical supply house. (Caution: Isopropyl alcohol is toxic if taken internally and it is flammable.)

COLD CREAM

Ingredients:

Mineral oil	2 cups

White beeswax	1/2 cup
Pyramid water	1 cup
Powdered borax	1-1/2 tablespoons

This is virtually the same as any commercial cold cream; use it to remove makeup and for general skin cleaning and conditioning. Put mineral oil and white beeswax into the top of double boiler and heat until the beeswax is melted, then allow it to cool down to 120° F. In a separate pan put 1 cup pyramid water and heat that to 120° F. Add 1-1/2 tablespoons powdered borax to the water and stir gently until it is dissolved. Then, very slowly , stirring all the while, pour the water and borax mixture into the oil and wax mixture. Cool until it just starts to solidify, and pour into containers.

Beeswax may be purchased at a hobby store; powdered borax from a grocery store or hardware store; and mineral oil from a chemical supply house. (Caution: Mineral oil is flammable. Undiluted powdered borax is toxic by ingestion. If, when used regularly, it causes a rash, discontinue use.)

ALLOVER SKIN CREAM

Ingredients:

Pyramid water	2 cups
White petrolatum	1 cup
Anhydrous lanolin	3/4 tablespoon
Glycerin	1 teaspoon

For a cream that you can use wherever you want to, on dry spots such as ankles, knees, and elbows, or whatnot, heat 1 cup white petrolatum and 3/4 tablespoon anhydrous lanolin in a double boiler. In a separate pan warm 2 cups pyramid water to which has been added 1 teaspoon glycerin. When both mixtures are warm, stir them together, cool until it just starts to solidify and add a few drops of a nonoil base perfume or essence if you

81

wish. (Caution: White petrolatum is flammable.)

You may obtain all the ingredients used in this formula from a drugstore.

ANTIPERSPIRANT LIQUID

Ingredients:

Denatured alcohol (type 40) or	
Isopropyl alcohol	1/2 cup
Pyramid water	2-1/2 cups
Powdered alum	1 tablespoon
Powdered zinc oxide	1 tablespoon

It has struck us as rather amusing that several commercial manufacturers have come out with an "unscented" version of their antiperspirants. If you're tired of spending all that money for those aerosol cans, which, by the way, are becoming an increasingly serious source of both air and solid waste pollution, it's easy to make your own. Mix the denatured or isopropyl alcohol with pyramid water, and thoroughly stir into it 1 tablespoon of powdered alum, and 1 tablespoon powdered zinc oxide. A plastic squeeze bottle that can be reused is perfect for storing this. Shake before using.

(Caution: Denatured and isopropyl alcohol are toxic and flammable.)

Zinc oxide may be purchased at a ceramic shop or drugstore; isopropyl alcohol, denatured alcohol and powdered alum may be obtained from a drugstore or chemical supply house.

FACE LOTION

Ingredients:

Glycerin	1/4 cup

Isopropyl alcohol	1-3/4 cups
Pyramid water	3 cups
Water soluble perfume	several drops

A clean clear complexion is an asset to anyone. But unfortunately our poor faces take such a beating from dozens of contaminants that we all need to give our skin special care.

As our air becomes more polluted our skin takes abuse. Oxides of nitrogen, sulfuric acid, and particulate matter such as the black smoke we see from diesel trucks, trains, and poorly maintained automobile engines all contribute to pollution as do dust and dirt. Dermatologists whom I have queried agree that as pollution increases, they are seeing more and more evidence of skin disorders. And the best preventive measure appears to be keeping the pores clean and free of contaminants.

Here's a formula that's easy and inexpensive to make and seems to do a good job. Mix the first three ingredients together while stirring. Add perfume if desired. Isopropyl alcohol has a mild, pleasant odor which may partially mask the perfume. However, as it evaporates from the skin the odor disappears leaving the perfume scent intact. To use, wash face thoroughly and then splash on face lotion. Store excess in glass or plastic containers. (Caution: Isopropyl alcohol is mildly toxic and flammable.)

Glycerin and isopropyl alcohol may be purchased at drugstores.

RUBBING ALCOHOL COMPOUND

Ingredients:

Denatured or isopropyl alcohol	1-3/4 cups
Glycerin	1/4 cup
Pyramid water	1/2 cup

Mix these three ingredients together, store in glass or plastic containers and keep containers tightly sealed to minimize loss by evaporation.

(Caution: Isopropyl alcohol is toxic and flammable.)

All ingredients listed for this formula may be obtained from a drugstore.

7

Pyramids for Gardening

CAUTION TO READERS

All chemicals that are stored in containers should be labeled, regardless of whether they are a raw material or a finished compound. This is basic, and must be followed in the interest of safety. Keep all chemicals out of the reach of children, and note the contents on the label. In this way if a child, or even an unsuspecting adult, should accidentally consume the contents, the doctor would know what treatment to initiate. While these formulas have been chosen with an eye to safety, many materials normally regarded as safe can be dangerous if taken internally, or to excess.

If the material is toxic by inhalation, use with adequate ventilation. If it is harmful by ingestion, call a physician or poison control center immediately if it has been ingested. If it is an irritant to skin, flush freely with water. If flammable, as are waxes and oils as well as other materials such as solvents, keep the chemical away from open flame or excessive heat.

Although high precision is not required, measurements should be accurate. Standard U.S. measuring spoons and measuring cups should be used. Teaspoons and tablespoons are level spoonfuls. The same is true for cups, half cups, and so on.

Here's an example of a safe label.

```
+-----------------------------------------------+
| This Bottle Contains _____ |
| Its Ingredient(s) are:                        |
|                                               |
|                                               |
|                                               |
| Keep out of reach of children.                |
|                                               |
| Made by _____ |
|                                               |
| Date _____ |
|            KEEP BOTTLE SEALED                 |
+-----------------------------------------------+
```

While many readers will buy their produce to dehydrate in a pyramid, many others will prefer to grow it themselves. Gardening is, in my opinion, a very rewarding hobby. Writing as I do, there is a need for exercise that this hobby fills. And the wonder of seeing tiny seeds mature into edible fruits and vegetables is a real thrill.

We feel that three of the most important factors in successful gardening are compost, which supplies humus to the soil, the pH (acidity or alkalinity) of the soil, and safe insecticides to control garden pests.

COMPOST MAKING

Mother nature has provided us with a closed system that is ecologically nearly perfect. A good example of this is the tree. The root system supplies water and nutrients, and when fall comes the leaves drop around the trunk and produce compost, which enhances the further growth of the tree during the next growing season. Unfortunately, man, having no real appreciation for this marvelous system, has come along and largely destroyed it. Instead of leaving it as nature intended, we rake up the leaves and burn them, polluting the atmosphere. But there is a way by which we can follow nature's plan and reap the rewards of lush growth and increased crop yields. That way is making and using compost. And, it's free.

Compost is partially decomposed organic material that can be returned to the earth to improve the productivity of the soil. It increases water-holding capacity and improves soil structure and drainage, which aids in the removal of harmful salts. The process of making compost utilizes organic waste materials giving them a positive value. Any organic material such as newspapers, paper boxes and bags, wood shavings and sawdust, leaves, grass clippings, and kitchen wastes can be used. Vegetative matter that originally had the benefit of pyramid

87

energy in some stage of its development will greatly enhance the value of your compost pile. But there are materials that can't be composted. Examples of these are glass, metal, plastics, crockery, bones, and wax-coated paper.

The process of composting is to provide the preferred bacteria with conditions ideally suited to permit them to reduce the mass to an odorless substance by decomposition. Air, and the correct amount of moisture are the two most essential elements. For this reason, the compost pile should be built on the *surface* of the ground, and *never in a pit*. Following are the procedures for successful composting.

The author's double compost bin

Turning the compost from first to second bin

Step 1: Contain the area where your compost pile will be with a fence that permits the circulation of the air and keeps the material from blowing away or being scattered by animals or birds. The fencing can be chicken wire, chain link, or snow fencing. Our preference is the snow fencing as it is inexpensive, flexible so it can be used as a gate, and attractive. (See photograph.)

Step 2: Next, make a flat top pile of composting material on the ground inside the fenced area. As previously mentioned, use any organic material such as kitchen wastes, paper, etc., and especially any pyramid energized vegetative matter. (In our operation we put waste materials in newspapers or paper bags before putting them on the pile as this eliminates the problem of flies.)

Step 3: After about 12 inches of composting material has been spread out in the bin, cover the entire surface with about 2 inches to 3 inches of garden soil or dehydrated manure which will provide the bacteria that causes decomposition. Then continue adding composting materials until another 12 inches has been built up, etc.

Step 4: Dampen pile, when possible with energized pyramid water. The amount of moisture you add to your compost pile is very important. The pile should be damp at all times, but never wet. And it should never have an objectionable odor. But if it does, it will be because of too much moisture. This will be your sign to back off on the amount of water.

Step 5: Composting can and should be a continuous process. So it is advisable to make your fencing cover an area sufficient in size to provide two bins, with a divider of snow fence between them. After your first pile has been allowed to build up, heat and decompose for about six weeks, it should be forked to the second bin. Thus the top layer of the first bin will become the bottom of the second bin. Now you can start to use the top layer of the second bin while a new supply is being built up in the first bin.

Step 6: Relatively large amounts of compost are need-

Leveling turned compost
pile in second bin

Moving finished compost
into garden area for mix-
ing into soil

ed to improve soil and it should be applied frequently, preferably before planting time. The method we find works best is to spread up to 6 inches of compost over the area, and work into the soil. (See photograph.)

Composting is a rewarding effort. With pyramid energized vegetative matter and pyramid water you are feeding into the soil some of the energy the pyramid has produced for you. Actually it's like getting something for nothing, in that wastes are converted to a usable product.

pH PREFERENCES OF SOME PLANTS

Let us assume that you have germinated your seeds in a pyramid. You have then enriched your soil with compost which is aided by pyramid energized materials. You will want to go on now to follow every step that will make your garden an extraordinary one. So while the following information doesn't directly involve the use of pyramids, it is included because it does make sense to take advantage of any practice that will increase yields for the same amount of effort. And one of the most rewarding things that can be easily done is to provide the plant with soil that has been adjusted to the most desirable degree of acidity or alkalinity. This is known as adjusting the pH of the soil.

For practical purposes the range of pH we are concerned with is from 4 to 8, with 7 representing neutral. As you go down the scale from 7, the acidity increases. As you go up the scale from 7, the alkalinity increases. The procedures for testing the pH of the soil are simple, and will be covered in another paragraph.

Now let's go through a typical example of adjusting the soil in a given area to make it ideal for the plants we wish to grow there. By reference to the following table, we find that asparagus, beets, cabbage, carrots, cauliflower, celery, lettuce, onions and parsley all have a pH preference range of 7 to 8 with the ideal being 7.5 on the scale, which is slightly alkaline. So naturally it follows that these vegetables should be planted in the same area where the soil has been adjusted to a pH of approximately 7.5. Of course, the same procedure applies to other areas where plants of other pH preferences will be grown. In the case of house plants, each pot of soil will be individually adjusted to the plant's preference.

To determine and alter soil pH, you will need an inexpensive tester. There are a number of these on the market that may be obtained from garden supply centers and swimming pool supply dealers. The writer's preference is to use chemically treated paper that changes color to indicate pH. This paper comes in rolls about 1/4-inch wide, housed in a plastic transparent-type dispenser. The procedure we use is as follows:

Step 1: Let's assume you have set aside an area 5 feet wide by 20 feet in length to grow the group of vegetables that prefer a pH of 7.5. Your objective is to adjust the soil in that area to a pH of approximately 7.5. First, get a glass container that will hold at least a pint of water. (A pyrex measuring cup works fine.) You will also need either a plastic or wooden spoon. Rinse the inside of the glass container and the spoon with distilled or demineralized water. These are commonly used for steam irons, and are available at any supermarket. Be sure your hands do not touch the inside of the glass or bowl of the spoon, as this could contaminate your reading.

Step 2: To obtain an average sample of the area in which you want to determine and adjust the pH, place a spoonful of soil taken from locations in the area about 3 feet apart, and several inches below the surface. Mix these samples together in the glass thoroughly. Next, cover the soil with distilled or demineralized water to about 1/2 inch over the soil. Now, using your spoon, mix the water and soil thoroughly and allow glass container to stand undisturbed. In a short time, the soil will settle to the bottom of the container leaving the clear water over it.

Step 3: You are now ready to determine what the pH of the area is. Pull out about a 2-inch strip of the chemically treated paper from the dispenser and hold by one end. Do not allow your fingers to come into contact with the rest of the paper strip. Immerse one end of the paper in the clear water over the soil and compare the wet section of the strip with the color chart found on the side of the container. The match of color between the strip and chart will tell you the pH of the soil.

Step 4: Formulas for adjusting the pH of house plants are not generally economical for larger areas such as gardens. For this use, the most effective and economical method is as follows: to alkalize the soil, i.e., to raise the pH number, the least expensive and best material to use is ground limestone. The formula is 6 pounds of limestone for each 100 square feet of area to increase the pH by one point. Therefore, if the pH of your soil is 6.5 and the desired level is 7.0, you would need to work in 3 pounds of limestone for the 100 square-foot area.

On the other hand, if the soil needed to be acidified, the formula would be to use either aluminum sulfate or powdered sulfur, whichever is lower in cost and most readily available in your area. Applied at the rate of 2 pounds for each 100 square feet of area, the pH will be lowered by one point on the scale. Thus, if your soil had a pH of 8 and you wanted 7.5, you would have to work in 1 pound of either material over the 100 square-foot area.

We are constantly adjusting soil pH on our research and testing facility near Tucson, Arizona, and find two methods of application to be effective. Either a small seed spreader with an adjustable discharge slot, or a rotary seeder or duster, also adjustable, will do a good job of giving even distribution over the area. After the material has been distributed, we work it into the soil with a roto-tiller. Of course, for small areas an ordinary garden rake will do just as well. It is important to remember that some time is required for the full acidifying or alkalizing process to complete itself. Therefore, the most desirable time to test and adjust is in the fall, and then make a final check before planting time.

Following is a list of vegetables, fruits, flowers, and grasses showing their acceptable pH range. The optimum value is at the midpoint of the range. For example, the acceptable range for asparagus is 7-8, so the optimum value is 7.5.

The First Practical Pyramid Book

Vegetables and Fruits

NAME	pH RANGE	pH OPTIMUM
Asparagus	7 — 8	7.5
Beets	7 — 8	7.5
Cabbage	7 — 8	7.5
Carrots	7 — 8	7.5
Cauliflower	7 — 8	7.5
Celery	7 — 8	7.5
Lettuce	7 — 8	7.5
Onions	7 — 8	7.5
Parsley	7 — 8	7.5
Plums	7 — 8	7.5
Broccoli	6 — 7	6.5
Brussels Sprouts	6 — 7	6.5
Corn	6 — 7	6.5
Cucumbers	6 — 7	6.5
Peas	6 — 7	6.5
Peppers	6 — 7	6.5
Radishes	6 — 7	6.5
Raspberries	6 — 7	6.5
Rhubarb	6 — 7	6.5
Spinach	6 — 7	6.5
Melons	6 — 7	6.5
Beans	5 — 6	5.5
Citrus	5 — 6	5.5
Parsnips	5 — 6	5.5
Potatoes	5 — 6	5.5
Grapes	5 — 6	5.5
Squash	5 — 6	5.5
Strawberries	5 — 6	5.5
Tomatoes	5 — 6	5.5
Turnips	5 — 6	5.5

Flowers

NAME	pH RANGE	pH OPTIMUM
Barberry	7 — 8	7.5
Calendula	7 — 8	7.5
Geranium	7 — 8	7.5

NAME	pH RANGE	pH OPTIMUM
Morning Glory	7 — 8	7.5
Nasturtium	7 — 8	7.5
Petunia	7 — 8	7.5
Poppy	7 — 8	7.5
Sweet Pea	7 — 8	7.5
Alyssum	6 — 7	6.5
Aster	6 — 7	6.5
Candytuft	6 — 7	6.5
Cauna	6 — 7	6.5
Carnation	6 — 7	6.5
Chrysanthemum	6 — 7	6.5
Columbine	6 — 7	6.5
Cosmos	6 — 7	6.5
Crocus	6 — 7	6.5
Dahlia	6 — 7	6.5
Dogwood	6 — 7	6.5
Feverfew	6 — 7	6.5
Gladiolas	6 — 7	6.5
Hollyhock	6 — 7	6.5
Hyacinth	6 — 7	6.5
Hydrangia (Pink)	6 — 7	6.5
Iris	6 — 7	6.5
Marigold	6 — 7	6.5
Pansy	6 — 7	6.5
Peony	6 — 7	6.5
Rose	6 — 7	6.5
Snapdragon	6 — 7	6.5
Tulip	6 — 7	6.5
Violet	6 — 7	6.5
Zinnia	6 — 7	6.5
Delphinium	5 — 6	5.5
Easter Lily	5 — 6	5.5
Fern	5 — 6	5.5
Lupine	5 — 6	5.5
Begonia	5 — 6	5.5
Phlox	5 — 6	5.5
Primrose	5 — 6	5.5

NAME	pH RANGE	pH OPTIMUM
Azalea	4 — 5	4.5
Holly	4 — 5	4.5
Hydrangia (Blue)	4 — 5	4.5
Rhododendron	4 — 5	4.5

Grasses

Blue Grass	7 — 8	7.5
Clover	7 — 8	7.5
Squirrel Tail Grass	7 — 8	7.5
Red Clover	6 — 7	6.5
Bermuda Grass	6 — 7	6.5
Colonial Bent Grass	6 — 7	6.5
Creeping Bent Grass	6 — 7	6.5
Italian Rye Grass	6 — 7	6.5
Perennial Rye Grass	6 — 7	6.5
Rough Blue Grass	6 — 7	6.5
Sudan Grass	5 — 6	5.5
Panic Grass	4 — 5	4.5

GROWING PLANTS IN A PYRAMID

While germinating seeds and growing seedlings in pyramids have been discussed in another section, a specific experiment run this past summer (1976) should be reported on because of the dramatic results.

This test was conducted at our Wisconsin facility located about 30 miles northwest of Milwaukee. Gladiola bulbs were purchased from a certified commercial grower and were hand-selected to be as nearly alike as possible.

The planting site was tilled and fertilized and the pH (acidity or alkalinity of the soil) adjusted to the pH preference of gladiolas, 6.5. The test area was then divided into three sections—all identical. The first, second, and third sections were each planted with 6 bulbs to identical depth and equally spaced as to distance apart.

Bulbs of gladiolas were planted on the same day. Gladiolas on the left were planted in the open air. Gladiolas in the center were planted in pyramid. Gladiolas on the right were planted in a box frame. The box was covered with the same material as the pyramid.

Section 1 had no covering of any kind. Section 2 was covered by a pyramid, and Section 3 covered by a box made of exactly the same cubic content as the pyramid.

On August 10, 1976, the faces of the pyramid and box were removed so a sharp photograph could be taken. The height of the tallest plants on that day were: 24 inches in Section 1, 54 inches in pyramid Section 2, and 36 inches in box Section 3. (See photograph.) There were no blooms on the plants in Sections 1 or 3, while the plants in pyramid Section 2 were in nearly full bloom with magnificent colors.

This experiment confirms the results of ones we have run here in Tucson, and leaves no doubt about the advantage of pyramid growing.

Because of space limitations in even a large-size pyramid, we don't feel it practical to grow plants to maturity

Lemon tree on left started as a seedling in the pyramid.

in it. The procedure we follow is to use it for germinating seeds and giving seedlings an advanced start before transplanting to the garden. As previously stated our experience is that starting in the pyramid reduces time to maturity by about one-third.

CONTROLLING GARDEN PESTS

Finally, even plants grown with the aid of pyramids require protection from those ever present garden pests. So we have provided some formulas for safe insecticides and repellents.

ALL PURPOSE GARDEN INSECTICIDE

Ingredients:
Pyrethrin extract   1 cup

Fuel oil   1 gallon

The Environmental Protection Agency (EPA) has banned many of the insecticides that have been widely used, such as chlordane, D.D.T., etc. So it's necessary to get down to some old proven basic ones. And this garden insecticide—all purpose—qualifies.

Mix the two ingredients listed above and stir thoroughly. Allow to stand for 48 hours and strain. Store in glass, impervious plastic, or metal containers. Spray leaves of plants to be protected but be cautious; the fuel oil could harm some delicate plants, so treat only one leaf as a test before spraying entire foliage. (Caution: Fuel oil is flammable and pyrethrin extract is toxic if taken internally. Use protective gloves when using the formula and discontinue use if it causes allergic reaction.) Fuel oil may be obtained from a service station or oil distributor; pyrethrin extract from a garden supply store.

JAPANESE BEETLE SPRAY

Ingredients:

Alum	3/4 cup
Hydrated lime	2 pounds
Water	10 gallons

These destructive insects have been brought fairly well under control, but there are still occasional problems with them in various parts of the country. To 10 gallons water add 2 pounds hydrated lime and 3/4 cup of alum, stirring until dissolved. Apply this with an agricultural sprayer, making sure that the undersides of the leaves are coated as well as the tops. (Caution: Hydrated lime is toxic, caustic and can cause burns. Use gloves and avoid inhalation.) Alum may be obtained from a drugstore; hydrated lime from a drugstore, feed and grain store, oil distributor, or chemical supply house.

PEA APHID SPRAY

Ingredients:

Sodium lauryl sulfate	1-1/2 teaspoons
Ground derris root	5 tablespoons
Water	5 gallons

Dissolve the sodium lauryl sulfate in water, then stir in the ground derris root. To use: apply with garden sprayer, especially to underside of leaves. Store in glass or impervious plastic containers. Sodium lauryl sulfate may be purchased at a drugstore or chemical supply house; ground derris root from a garden supply shop.

ANT REPELLENT

Ingredients:

Sassafras leaves	2 tablespoons
Water	2 cups

Have you ever wondered, as I have, what possible good can come from pests that seem to serve no purpose other than to annoy us? I've never known what possible reason God had for putting them on our planet earth. The common rat is a good example. Why are they here? What good do they do? None that I know of. They contaminate and destroy causing billions of dollars of damage each year. But I also wonder this. If by a magic formula all rats could be destroyed, would we then discover the reason for their being put here in the first place? Your guess is as good as mine.

But to the subject of ants. I'm not smart enough to know why they're here, but I prefer not to have them devour my garden, so here's a formula that I use to repel them and send them on their way.

Boil the sassafras leaves in the water for 5 minutes, cool and strain. Paint the liquid in any runways. It will send them on their way. Store liquid in glass or plastic containers. Sassafras leaves may be obtained from a drugstore or chemical supply house.

ANT MOUND ERADICATOR

Ingredients:

Pyrethrin extract	1 tablespoon
Liquid soap or detergent	1 cup
Water	8 gallons

To 8 gallons of water, add 1 cup liquid soap, then the pyrethrin extract, stirring well. Pour one cup on each ant mound, and repeat after an hour to make sure that the mixture penetrates down into all the galleries and tunnels in the soil. This formula may be cut in half if you desire to make a smaller quantity. Pyrethrin extract may be purchased from a garden supply store; the soap from a grocery store.

(Caution: Pyrethrin extract is toxic if taken internally. Use protective gloves when making and using the formula and discontinue use if it causes allergic reaction.)

CATERPILLAR AND INSECT TREE BANDS

Ingredients:

Powdered rosin	1-1/2 cups
Linseed oil	1 cup
Beeswax	1 tablespoon

Moths and butterflies are amazing insects found in all parts of the world. Of more than one hundred thousand identified species, approximately ten thousand are native to the United States. Wing spans range from over a foot in the Indian Atlas Moth to the minute span of the Gilded Moth—less than the diameter of the head of a pin.

The breathtaking beauty of many moths and butter-flies results from white, black, red, and yellow pigments in the scales found on the wings. Overlapping scales which work as prisms to break up light rays account for the blues, greens, and iridescent metallic shades. But don't be lulled into false security by all this beauty. While moths and butterflies are harmless to your garden, sex comes along and "rears its ugly head." Then they lay eggs and all h--- breaks loose. From the eggs, larvae, such as caterpillars, hatch with a full blown appetite for tender green things such as tiny new leaves on trees and shrubs. So if you're looking forward to shade from big leaves in the summer, it's wise to protect the little ones in the spring. This can be easily and inexpensively done by painting caterpillar tree bands around the trunks. Here's how you do it.

Put all three ingredients together in the top of a dou-ble boiler (never over direct heat), heat and stir until melted and mixed. When cooled, transfer to a metal, im-pervious plastic, or glass container. To use, paint a band about 3 inches wide around the trunk of the tree to be protected. Powdered rosin may be obtained from a drug-store or chemical supply house; linseed oil from a hard-ware or paint store; beeswax from a drugstore or hobby shop. (Warning: Linseed oil dries when exposed to air. Keep in airtight container.)

RABBIT REPELLENT

Ingredients:

Hydrated lime	2 pounds
Calcium carbonate	1 pound

Rabbits are one of the most common of all American

game animals. This, coupled with the fact that they are delicious to eat, probably accounts for the fact that more sportsmen hunt rabbits than any other game.

The reproductive capacity of these cute little animals is well known. Breeding begins at about six months of age, and they have litters of from eight to twelve rabbits twice a year. (You engineer readers, get out your calculators and computers and do a little geometric progression. You'll be amazed at the numbers.) Now all this proliferating can't help but create healthy appetites as Mr. McGregor discovered in dealing with Peter, in his cabbage patch. So if you're having the same problem, here's a formula that will send the little freeloaders on their way.

Dry mix the above ingredients together. Store in metal, impervious plastic, or glass containers. To use: sprinkle powder around the base of the plants to be protected. Calcium carbonate may be obtained from a drugstore or county and state highway departments; hydrated lime from a drugstore, chemical supply house, or feed and grain store. (Caution: Hydrated lime is toxic, caustic and can cause burns. Use gloves and avoid inhalation.)

NICOTINE PEST KILLER—ALL PURPOSE

Ingredients:
Pipe tobacco
   (cheapest grade)   3 ounces
Water   1 gallon

Tie pipe tobacco in cloth bag and soak in water overnight. To use: spray top and underside of leaves. (Caution: This mixture is toxic if taken internally.) Pipe tobacco can be purchased at any drugstore.

night. To use: spray top and underside of leaves. (Caution: This mixture is toxic if taken internally.) Pipe tobacco can be purchased at any drugstore.

8

Pyramids for Dehydration

CAUTION TO READERS

In dehydrating food, utmost care should be taken to see that conditions are clean from start to finish. Wash hands often with soap and water. Don't handle food if you have sores on your face, hands, or arms. Keep tables, counters, cutting surfaces, knives, and other equipment scrupulously clean. Shield foods from insects at all times.

The efficacy of your pyramid in dehydration may depend on the temperature and humidity conditions in the area in which it is situated. Sustained heat and low humidity are the best conditions for drying foods. Cooler temperatures coupled with low humidity are the next best conditions. In areas of normally high humidity pyramid drying may be done in only a limited way, when favorable conditions exist. If drying takes more than thirty-six hours the possibility of mold is increased.

The safe maximum percentages of water to leave in home-dried produce are no more than 5 percent for vegetables and no more than 20 percent for fruit. You may therefore do a weight check for dryness. Ten ounces of fresh vegetables should weigh one-half ounce when fully dried. Ten ounces of fruit should weigh two ounces when fully dry.

Always check dehydrated food particularly meat and other proteins both before and after storage to be certain there is no mold or infestation, no off odor, and no rancidity. Any foods that show any of these properties should be immediately discarded!

Here are general directions for using free energy as an easy, economical way of dehydrating fruits, vegetables, meats, fish and poultry without artificial additives.

The advantages of pyramid dehydration should be considered by anyone concerned about health and the soaring costs of foods. And doesn't this include everyone? Our bodies are being assaulted more and more by additives that are used to preserve and enhance the flavors of the foods we eat. If we don't need artificial additives—why use them? If the following simple directions for dehydrating in a pyramid are carefully followed, the foods will be nutritious, economical, free of unwanted bacteria, and the flavors considerably enhanced.

The dehydration is accomplished by unknown electrical forces within the pyramid. Science has not been able to identify these forces, but we know that bodies placed, without treatment, centuries ago in the pyramids have become dehydrated or mummified. What is this energy? Perhaps we will never know, and if the sphinx guarding the great pyramids knows, she will never tell. The important thing is that this energy is free, and it constitutes a source needed for dehydration.

The trays used for dehydration of foods should be made of aluminum (energized) or nonmetallic screening tightly stretched over a frame of wood, and raised with one-inch legs to allow for an adequate circulation of air. The area of highest energy in the pyramid is slightly above the level of the King's Chamber. And ideally, if a large pyramid is available, all trays should be placed on a shelf at this level. We have found, however, that although the foods may require a slightly longer drying time, they do dehydrate well in other areas. The owner of a small pyramid may stack a series of trays, with the bottom tray on casters, and simply slide the stack into the pyramid. Provide for ventilation as shown for the miniature pyramid at the back of this book.

Select fruits and vegetables for dehydration that are as freshly picked as possible. Use the harvest from your own garden, or buy produce directly from the growers or from a local farmers' market. The fresher the foods, the better the results will be; and by using the produce at the peak of its growing season the cost will be low—adding sunshine to your budget. In preparing the foods keep in mind the principles of cleanliness. All utensils should be clean, and a plastic cutting board is preferable to a wooden one. A wooden board may harbor a myriad of bacteria even though well scrubbed; whereas a plastic board is not porous, and will not absorb and retain decomposing food particles. The drying trays should be washed and dried and carefully stored after each use. The pyramid and its floor and shelves should be clean and free of flies or insects of any kind. All produce should be thoroughly washed, and inferior portions discarded.

When blanching of vegetables is indicated, steam-blanch by placing the vegetables in a steamer, colander or basket over boiling water. Cover tightly and keep the water boiling until each piece is thoroughly heated through. Steam blanching is preferred to boiling, as less nutrients will be lost, the vegetables will not be water-logged, and a better color will be retained.

After steaming, drain the vegetables, or place them on paper towels to absorb excess moisture. Immediately spread the vegetables in a single layer on the aluminum (energized) screened drying trays, and place the trays in the pyramid where they will be slightly above the King's Chamber surface. If the pyramid is small and multiple trays are to be used, stack the trays, placing the tray with the casters on the bottom, and simply roll the stack into the pyramid.

When blanching is not required, wash the fruits or vegetables, drain well, or put on paper towels to remove excess moisture. Then proceed with the dehydration instructions as given for blanched foods.

Many fruits are briefly put into a salt-water solution of one teaspoonful of salt to one quart of water to retard discoloration. These fruits are to be thoroughly drained, or placed on paper towels and patted dry. Put these foods on the drying screens and place in the pyramid, following the instructions for dehydrating blanched and unblanched foods.

Some vegetables, such as green beans, will bleach out if placed in a sunny spot in the pyramid. To prevent this, cover the trays with black gauze. Black crepe paper may be used if it is slightly elevated from the vegetables, thus preventing the color from the paper bleeding into the food.

The drying times will depend upon the variables in the geographic locations of the pyramids, and also upon the density and moisture content of the foods. Most foods dry satisfactorily within twenty-four to seventy-two hours; however, some experimentation will be necessary by the individual pyramid owner.

Since water causes the bacteria in food to grow, enough of it should be removed to prevent the foods from spoiling. Vegetables to be used for the table should be dehydrated until fairly crisp. The ones that are to be ground or powdered should be extra crisp. Fruits should be dehydrated to the point of being rubbery and chewable; yet they should not feel moist on the outside. As an extra safety precaution it is recommended that foods, after being dehydrated in the pyramid, be pasteurized by spreading on trays and placing into a 150° F. oven for one-half hour. Put the cooled, dried foods into plastic bags, tightly sealed, or into airtight glass or plastic containers. Store in a cool, dry place. If any moisture or condensation appears in the plastic bag or container it indicates that not enough moisture has been removed and mold could occur. Remove the product from the container and return it to the pyramid for further dehydration. The product may then be repackaged for storage. If mold or infestation should appear at any time, discard the product!

The reconstitution of foods is simple, and may be accomplished by allowing the dried foods to stand in water, wine, fruit juice, tomato juice, or whatever liquid may be suitable to the food being reconstituted. Most foods can be quickly reconstituted by dropping them into boiling liquid and simmering until tender. Some experimentation will be needed for the amounts of liquid to be used. As a rule, two to three times as much liquid as dehydrated food is the proper ratio for reconstitution.

Imagination is the key to dehydration. The cost is low, the effort is minimal, and the results are excellent.

DEHYDRATING VEGETABLES

Asparagus

There are about 150 species of asparagus growing, native from Siberia to southern Asia and in the United States. Of all these, garden asparagus is of the greatest economic importance. It is grown in most temperate climates, and it is estimated that commercial growers produce about 175 tons from about 150,000 acres. A good portion of this volume is sold as fresh produce; the balance is preserved by canning or freezing.

One-hundred grams (about 3-1/2 ounces) of asparagus contains 20 calories, 2 grams protein, a trace of fat and 4 grams carbohydrate.

DEHYDRATING:
Select freshly harvested, tender spears of asparagus. Cut off and discard the woody lower part of the stalk. Remove the tips to be prepared as a table vegetable, leaving the center portion of the stems to be used for cream soups or as an addition to gravies and stews.

Separate the tips from the center portions of the asparagus, and steam-blanch both sections by placing in a steamer, colander or basket over boiling water. Cover tightly and keep the water boiling until each piece is thoroughly heated through. After steaming, drain the asparagus, or place the pieces on paper towels to absorb excess moisture. Immediately spread the asparagus in single layers on the (energized) screened aluminum drying trays and place the trays in the pyramid where they will be slightly above the surface of the King's Chamber. If a large amount of asparagus is to be dehydrated and the pyramid is small, use multiple trays. Spread the asparagus on the trays and stack them, placing a tray with casters on the bottom, and roll the entire stack into the pyramid. Drying time will depend upon the variables in different geographic locations. Put the dehydrated asparagus into sealable plastic bags and seal tightly, or into airtight glass or plastic containers. Store in a cool, dry place.

TO RECONSTITUTE:

Place the asparagus tips in cold water, using the ratio of 1 cup of asparagus to 2 cups of water. Or drop the tips into boiling water, reduce the heat and simmer until tender. Season and serve. The dried center portion of the stalks should be ground in a food processor or blender.

The following recipes are typical formulas for preparing dehydrated asparagus:

BAKED ASPARAGUS

Ingredients:

2   cups reconstituted asparagus tips
3   tablespoons melted butter
1   tablespoon reconstituted diced onion
2   tablespoons grated Parmesan cheese
1/4   cup bread crumbs
1/2   teaspoon salt
1/8   teaspoon pepper

Procedure:

Put melted butter in baking dish. Line bottom with asparagus. Mix all other ingredients together and spread evenly over the tips. Bake 45 minutes in 350° F. oven. If the tips were reconstituted by boiling, leave the dish in the oven just long enough for the mixture to be heated through.

CREAM OF ASPARAGUS SOUP

Ingredients:

1	cup ground asparagus
6	cups soup stock or chicken broth
3	tablespoons butter
3	tablespoons flour
1/2	cup cream
1/2	teaspoon salt

Procedure:

In a saucepan stir the ground asparagus into 5 cups

Rack of drying trays on casters in the pyramid

of cold stock or broth. Bring the mixture to a simmer and cook gently for 20 minutes. Make a smooth sauce of the flour blended with 1 cup of stock or broth; gradually add the sauce to the soup, stirring all the while. Add butter, cream, and salt. Reheat, but do not boil. To enhance the flavor of this soup, dehydrated celery leaves or onions may be added to the ground asparagus.

Beets

Garden beets were developed from the leaf beet about the beginning of the Christian era. They are now grown commercially in Europe, the United States, and Canada. In the United States about 20,000 acres are planted each year, producing up to 200,000 tons. One-hundred grams (about 3-1/2 ounces) of garden beets contain 35 calories, 1 gram protein, a trace of fat, and 9 grams carbohydrates.

DEHYDRATING:
Thoroughly scrub the beets, leaving the roots and 1 inch of the stems. Steam the whole beets for 5 minutes, then to facilitate peeling, drop the beets into cold water. Cut into 1/4-inch slices or squares. Spread in a single layer on the aluminum (energized) drying screen and place in the pyramid slightly above the King's Chamber. If necessary, use multiple drying screens. Spread the beets on screens and stack them; placing a screen with casters on the bottom, and roll the entire stack into the pyramid. Drying time will depend upon the variables in different geographic locations. Put the dehydrated beets into sealable plastic bags, or into airtight glass or plastic containers. Store in a cool, dark, dry place.

TO RECONSTITUTE:
Cook in boiling water until tender, season and serve. Or the beets may be dropped into cold water. For both

methods use the ratio of 1 cup of beets to 2 cups water. The following recipes are typical formulas for using dehydrated beets.

HARVARD BEETS

Reconstitute beets by cooking in water.
Ingredients:
2   cups cooked cubed or sliced beets
1   tablespoon cornstarch
4   teaspoons sugar
1/2   teaspoon salt
2/3   cup water in which the beets were cooked
1/4   cup vinegar

Procedure:
Mix cornstarch and seasonings in a saucepan. Blend cold beet water and vinegar into the cornstarch mixture. Slowly bring to a boil to thicken, stirring constantly. Add beets, reheat and serve.

PICKLED BEETS

Reconstitute beets by cooking in water, reserve the water. Use the ratio of approximately 1 cup of dehydrated beets to 2 cups of water.
Ingredients:
4   cups reconstituted sliced beets
1-1/2 cups cider vinegar
1-1/2 teaspoons dry mustard
1/4   teaspoon salt
1-1/4 cups sugar
1/2   cup reconstituted onions (approximately 1/4-cup dry)
2   teaspoons celery seed

Procedure:
Drain beets, retaining any liquid remaining. Heat the

Dehydrated carrots

vinegar, add beet liquid with additional water to make one cup of liquid. Bring to a boil. Mix the mustard, salt and sugar. Add the vinegar and let boil again. Put the beets and onions into clean canning jars. Add the celery seed and cover with the hot vinegar mixture. Seal, cool, and store in the refrigerator. The beets will keep for weeks.

Carrots

Carrots were originally native to Afghanistan and neighboring areas. They were cultivated in the Mediterranean region before the Christian era, and in China, France, and Germany by the thirteenth century. The colonists brought them to America.

115

Carrots are tap roots that consist of two sections—the center, called the wood or pith section, and the outer, known as cortex, where the food and vitamin values are stored.

Carotene is a pigment found in abundance in the cortex area of carrots. It is the most active pro-vitamin A, because its molecule contains two rings of the type found in vitamin A molecule. The human body has the ability to convert carotene to vitamin A. In 1920, the value of carotene in the human diet was recognized, greatly stimulating the commercial production of the crop.

A one-hundred-gram portion (about 3-1/2 ounces) of carrots will contain 42 calories, 1 gram protein, a trace of fat, and 9 grams of carbohydrates.

DEHYDRATING:

Scrub carrots thoroughly with a brush. To save valuable nutrients, do not peel. Trim both ends and cut in 1/4-inch slices or cubes. Steam-blanch the carrots by placing in a steamer, colander, or basket over boiling water. Cover tightly and keep the water boiling until each piece is thoroughly heated through. After steaming, drain the carrots, or place the pieces on paper towels to absorb excess moisture. Immediately spread the carrots on the aluminum (energized) drying screens and place in the pyramid where they will be slightly above the surface of the King's Chamber. If necessary, use multiple drying screens. Spread the carrots on the screens and stack them; placing a screen with casters on the bottom, and roll the entire stack into the pyramid. Drying time will depend upon the variables in different geographical locations. Put the dehydrated carrots into sealable plastic bags, or into airtight glass or plastic containers. Store in a cool, dark, dry place.

TO RECONSTITUTE:

Soak the carrots in approximately double the amount of water as carrots; or drop them into boiling water, cook until tender, drain, season and serve. The following is a typical formula for using dehydrated carrots.

GLAZED CARROTS

Cook a sufficient amount—approximately 1 cup of dehydrated carrots—to equal 4 whole carrots. Simmer in lightly salted water until just tender.

Ingredients:

4   cooked carrots
1   tablespoon honey
1/2 tablespoon of parsley, may be dehydrated
1   tablespoon butter
Salt to taste
Dash of lemon juice

Procedure:

To the hot cooked carrots add the honey, parsley and butter. Add salt, if necessary. Cook gently over a low heat until all ingredients are well blended. Add a dash of lemon juice and serve.

Corn (Sweet)

Corn, often referred to as "the grain that built a hemisphere," is native to America and was unknown to other countries until about 1492 with the exception of Mexico, Canada, and some South American countries.

Corn was a very important staple in the diet of both the North and South American Indians. There is much evidence to indicate that the North American Indians taught the early explorers how to grow and use corn. This knowledge spread around the world, and corn became one of the most important food sources that man has.

Sweet corn is one of the most extensively grown and

117

used vegetables in the United States. As compared to other types, it can be identified by its wrinkled translucent seeds. This results from the fact that the sugar manufactured by the plant is not converted to starch as it is in other types.

A 100-gram portion (about 3-1/2 ounces) contains 91 calories, 3 grams protein, 1 gram fat and 21 grams carbohydrates.

DEHYDRATING:

All corn dries well on the cob in the pyramid, and corn for popping is easily removed from the cob as it is needed. We have found, however, that the kernels of the corn to be used for the table are best removed before dehydration.

Select freshly picked, slightly immature cobs of sweet

In the foreground, cob corn hung in pyramid; left to right, kernel corn, peas, lima beans, and green cut beans

corn. Strip the husks and silk from the corn, and remove any inferior kernels. Leaving the corn on the cob, steam-blanch the corn in boiling water until it is well heated through. Cool the cobs under cold water, cut off the kernels with a sharp knife. Spread the corn on the aluminum (energized) drying screen and place in the pyramid where it will be slightly above the level of the King's Chamber. If the pyramid is small and you have a large amount of corn to dehydrate, use multiple drying screens. Although the area slightly above the King's Chamber is the highest energy level in the pyramid, we have found that foods do dry well in other areas. Spread the corn on the screens, stack them, placing the screen with the casters on the bottom, and roll the entire stack into the pyramid. Always be sure that your pyramid is correctly ventilated by following the instructions in this book for the ventilation of small pyramids. The drying time will depend on variables in different geographic locations. Put into sealable plastic bags, or airtight glass or plastic containers. Store in a cool, dry place.

TO RECONSTITUTE:

Corn will dry thoroughly and it is best to reconstitute it by soaking in water overnight. Approximately twice as much water as corn will be needed. A wonderful memory from my childhood is reconstituted corn, simmered until tender and seasoned with butter, salt and pepper.

Following are typical formulas for using dehydrated sweet corn:

CORN AND GREEN PEPPERS

Ingredients:
3   cups reconstituted sweet corn
1   tablespoon chopped green peppers
3   tablespoons butter
4   tablespoons cream
Seasoning to taste

119

Procedure:
Simmer slowly, in a small amount of water, the re-constituted sweet corn. When tender, drain, add the remaining ingredients and cook just until the peppers are tender. Season with salt and pepper and serve.

CORN FRITTERS

As youngsters we called these fritters, "Mother's Friday Night Special."
Ingredients:
2   eggs—separated
3   tablespoons milk
2   tablespoons flour
1/2 teaspoon salt
2   cups reconstituted corn

Procedure:
Strain corn and add beaten egg yolks. Stir in the rest of the ingredients, folding in the stiffly beaten egg whites last. Drop by tablespoonsful into deep, hot cooking oil heated to 350° F. When fritters are lightly browned, remove from the fat and drain on paper towels. Serve with syrup, applesauce or powdered sugar.

Onions

The onion, a vegetable native to middle Asia, has been cultivated since prehistoric times. It is now grown the world over and it is one of our best loved and most used foods. The Spanish and the Bermuda onions are popularly grown crops; and they produce a firm fleshed bulb that dries, keeps well in cool storage, and is highly desired as a food, either cooked or raw. Non-bulbing onions, what we usually refer to as "green bunching onions," can be harvested any time they are large enough

From left to right, dehydrating green onion tops, onion rings, and chopped onions

to eat. Bulbing onions can be gathered in a like manner, before the mature bulbs form, and used immediately. These onions are marketed with the fresh green tops attached, and the tops are excellent as a delectable, colorful flavoring. Onions are versatile, and a wise cook will always keep a good supply of them on hand.

DEHYDRATING:

There are four methods of dehydration depending upon what portion of the onion is to be used: (1) drying the whole onion for winter storage; (2) drying thin slices of onion, such as might be used in preparing onion rings; (3) dicing the onion; (4) drying the green tops.

1. Drying the whole onion does not produce the same degree of dehydration as when it is peeled and cut. However, pyramid drying removes substantially more mois-

121

ture than does ordinary air drying. The result is appreciably longer storage periods without refrigeration.

In drying the whole onions do not remove the tops. Tie the tops into bunches and hang them in the pyramid, slightly above the level of the King's Chamber. After drying, cut off the tops and store the onions in a cool, dark, dry, well ventilated area.

2. In dehydrating slices of onions, the bulb should be peeled and washed. Cut off the pithy section on each end and slice into 1/4-inch thick sections. Spread slices on energized aluminum screen wire and place about one inch above the King's Chamber level. As explained in (1), drying of the whole onion with the peel left on retains a substantial amount of water; so if the onions are sliced or cubed, the drying time will naturally be greatly reduced. Dehydrate until the onions are crisp-dried. Place in airtight containers, and store in a cool, dark, dry place.

3. If dehydrated onions are to be used in soups, salads, etc., they should be diced. And from this form they can be easily ground into a powder in a blender or food processor. In this case, dice the slices to about 1/4-inch sections, place on energized aluminum screen wire about an inch above the King's Chamber level. Thoroughly dry the onions, put them into airtight containers and store in a cool, dark, dry place.

4. Onion tops (greens) are great in dishes such as salads and soups. They dehydrate and retain their flavor beautifully. The tops used should be taken from the bulbing onions before they mature, or the tops of green bunching onions can be used in the same manner. Cut into 1/4-inch sections and place on an energized screen about 1 inch above the King's Chamber level. These onions will dehydrate quickly. Place into plastic bags, tightly sealed, or into airtight plastic or glass containers. Store in a cool, dark, dry place.

A 100-gram portion (about 3-1/2 ounces) contains 38 calories, 2 grams protein, a trace of fat, and 9 grams carbohydrate.

TO RECONSTITUTE:

Onion cubes and slices may be reconstituted by allowing them to stand in cold water. Use approximately 1 cup of onions to 2 cups of water. The green onion tops will also reconstitute well in water.

Following are typical formulas for using dehydrated onions:

ONION AND GARLIC POWDER

Ingredients:
Dehydrated onions   amount desired
Dehydrated garlic   amount desired

Procedure:

Use crisply dried onions and garlic. Grind the two together in a blender or food processor. Add salt if desired. Use as a condiment on meats, in cooked dishes, or wherever a zesty flavor is desired.

ONION GREENS

Reconstitute in cold water for use in salads, dips, cottage cheese, or as a garnish on meats and vegetables. Drop the dehydrated onion greens directly into simmering soups or stews.

SLICED OR CUBED DEHYDRATED ONIONS

After the onions have been reconstituted they can be used in any recipe that calls for the addition of this flavorsome vegetable. They can be used for preparing creamed onions or they can be lightly sautéed in butter and used as an accompaniment to meats. For use in gravies, soups or stews, they may be included dehydrated or reconstituted when the dish is prepared, or they can be dropped in towards the end of the cooking period.

FRENCH ONION SOUP

Ingredients:
6   cups beef broth
1   cup sliced dehydrated onions
3   tablespoons butter
1/4   cup sherry, if desired
6   slices toasted bread
1/2   cup grated Parmesan cheese
Salt to taste

Procedure:
Bring the broth to a boil. A little Kitchen Bouquet may be added to darken the color of the soup. Add dehydrated onions. Simmer gently until the onions are tender. If desired, add sherry. Salt to taste. Toast the bread, cut it into cubes and put into soup plates. Cover with 2 tablespoons cheese. Pour soup into plates over the toasted bread, and serve with additional cheese.

Garlic

Garlic is a bulbous plant native to Asia, and now grown in the United States, chiefly in California. The bulb consists of small sections called cloves which are peeled, then used chopped, whole or are pressed to obtain the oil for flavoring.

DEHYDRATING:
Leave the top on the garlic. Tie in bunches and hang in the pyramid. Drying time will depend on the variables in different geographic locations. Place dehydrated garlic in plastic bags and seal tightly. Store in a cool, dark place.

For garlic powder, peel garlic cloves, and dice into small pieces. Place diced garlic evenly on energized aluminum screen trays about 1 inch above the King's Chamber level. Drying time will depend on the variables in different geographic locations.

GARLIC POWDER

Grind the dehydrated diced garlic cloves in a blender or food processor. Salt (to taste) may be added after grinding. Store powder in tightly covered containers. But when you've eaten this delicious condiment, be sure your friends have too, or you might be quite lonesome.

Peppers

Deadly Nightshade is a highly poisonous plant to humans. Peppers are members of the Nightshade family, and while they're not poisonous, of course, a "hot one" can bring tears to the eyes.

The fleshy varieties range from mild to hot and include the Pungent Cherry, Cone, Tabasco, Red Cluster, Hot Chili, Cayenne, Bell, and Sweet Peppers such as are used in salads and other dishes.

One of the most beautiful drives I have ever made was on the old highway that runs along the Rio Grande south from Albuquerque to Las Cruces, New Mexico. Here pepper fields cover the entire river basin for as far as you can see. Interspersed between the miles of pepper fields are small packing plants where the peppers are processed for marketing worldwide.

Here in the Southwest the use of peppers is a way of life. Ranging from mild to hot, they are used in many dishes, and have decorative value as well. In many homes, strings of colorful red chili peppers may be found hanging in kitchens, on patios and from fireplace mantles. They are removed from the string as needed, to be replaced by new strings from the next harvest. A 100-gram portion (about 3-1/2 ounces) of peppers contains 25

Dehydrating string of whole pods of red chili peppers. String is hung from pyramid.

calories, 1 gram protein, trace of fat and 5 grams carbohydrate.

There are several types of hot peppers used for seasonings, as well as various sweet peppers used for general cooking. Following will be found the preparation and dehydrating instructions for one of each.

DEHYDRATING RED CHILI PEPPERS:

Select mature pods, but do not remove the stems. Wash thoroughly and dry with a clean cloth or paper towels. No treatment is necessary. String the whole pods by running a needle and heavy cord through the stems. Hang the peppers, stem end up, in the pyramid. Dry until the pods are shrunken, flexible and dark red. Because these peppers do not readily pick up moisture from air as many other vegetables do, the strings can merely be hung for storage anywhere there is a good circulation of air. Hanging them in the pyramid, however, will greatly shorten the drying time.

To use these peppers for cooking, remove them as needed, when they are thoroughly dry. Wash and dry before preparing. To use as chili powder, remove the seeds and grind the peppers to a fine powder in a blender, grinder or food processor. For spicy, hot dishes, coarse grind the entire pepper, without removing the seeds. For sauces, or salsa, mix the ground peppers with stewed tomatoes, tomato paste or sauce. Add additional water if needed for the proper consistency. Use as much ground pepper as you like, depending upon the flavor and spiciness you desire.

DEHYDRATING SWEET GREEN BELL PEPPERS:

Select firm, fresh peppers. Wash and dry the peppers, and remove the stem and seeds. Slice them into strips 1/4-inch wide, or cut them into squares. Place the peppers on an aluminum (energized) drying screen and put the screen into the pyramid, slightly above the King's Chamber level. The drying time will depend upon the variables

127

Reconstituting dried foods

in different geographic locations. When dehydrated, put the peppers into plastic bags, tightly sealed, or into air-tight plastic or glass containers. Store in a cool, dark, place.

TO RECONSTITUTE:
Cover the peppers with approximately double the amount of water as peppers and allow to stand; or drop the dehydrated peppers directly into the foods as they are being cooked.

PEPPER RELISH

Ingredients:
1   dehydrated red chili pepper with seeds

128

1   cup diced dehydrated green pepper
1   cup diced dehydrated onion
2   cups vinegar
2   cups water
1   teaspoon salt
1   teaspoon mustard seed
1/2   cup sugar

Procedure:

Grind dehydrated red chili pepper, leaving in seeds if a hot relish is desired. Mix with onions and green pepper. Combine vinegar, water, salt and mustard seeds and bring to a rolling boil. Pour over peppers and onions and let stand until ingredients are reconstituted. Reheat to a boil. Bottle and seal.

Following are some typical formulas for using dehydrated peppers:

CHILI CON CARNE

Ingredients:
1   pound ground beef
2   teaspoons fat
1/2   teaspoon paprika
2   teaspoons ground dehydrated chili peppers
1   cup dehydrated kidney beans
2   cups tomatoes
1/4   cup dehydrated onion (cubed)
1   cup water
Salt to taste

Procedure:

Reconstitute kidney beans by soaking in water overnight. Brown ground beef in hot fat. Add peppers, onions, tomatoes, paprika, ground chili peppers and water. Cook until all ingredients are tender, then add the kidney beans. Simmer until flavors are well blended.

NOTE: The amount of chili peppers can be varied depending on how hot you like your Chili Con Carne.

Zucchini

Zucchini, a summer squash, grows from bushy plants and develops into a cylindrical, straight to slightly curved vegetable, with dark green skin and creamy white, tender flesh. It is ready for table use when the squash is from 5 inches to 12 inches long. The plants grow luxuriously and a generous crop can be obtained from 2 or 3 plants. They will also reseed themselves from year to year, and some years, to my chagrin, we have found the tenacious vines presenting themselves, uninvited and unwanted throughout our garden. My wife just laughs, as zucchini is her favorite vegetable, and she says she does it with her "garden hex." And this is not her only "hexability."

DEHYDRATING:
Wash the zucchini, cut off the stems, but do not peel. Cut into slices 1/4-inch thick. Steam-blanch the slices until heated through, and when drained, dip them into cold salt water, using 1 teaspoon of salt to a quart of water to cool and prevent discoloration. Drain well, or place the zucchini on paper towels to dry. Immediately place the slices on the aluminum (energized) drying screens and put them into the pyramid, slightly above the level of the King's Chamber. If necessary, use multiple drying screens and roll the entire stack into the pyramid. The drying time will depend upon the variables in different geographic locations. Put the dehydrated zucchini into plastic bags, tightly sealed, or into glass or plastic airtight containers. Store in a cool, dark, dry place.

TO RECONSTITUTE:
Cover the zucchini with cold water and allow to stand approximately 4 hours, or drop the zucchini into boiling

water and let simmer until just tender. Do not overcook. Drain thoroughly and season with salt, pepper and butter. Following are formulas for the use of zucchini:

DIPS

Zucchini chips are delicious when used as dippers, or as the basis for appetizer spreads, i.e., cream cheese mixed with Roquefort cheese or with reconstituted diced onions, or green onion tops.

ZUCCHINI WITH SOUR CREAM
OR
CARELESS CALORIES

Ingredients:
2   cups reconstituted or very lightly cooked zucchini
1   cup sour cream
1/4   cup buttered bread crumbs
Salt and pepper to taste

Procedure:
Drain zucchini well, and mix gently with the sour cream and the seasonings. Place the mixture in a small casserole and sprinkle with the buttered bread crumbs. Pop into a 325° F. oven for 20 minutes.

Potatoes

The common potato, a tuber, its name derived from the Spanish patata, is one of the eight main food crops of the world. It is considered to be a native of the Peruvian-Bolivian Andes, and proof exists of its being cultivated there as early as the second century A.D. The potato became well known to English-speaking people by the end of the seventeenth century.

131

The dry content of the freshly dug tuber averages about 25 percent, and consists of 70–75 percent starch; 0.5 percent to 1 percent sugar; 1–2 percent nitrogen; 0.02–0.04 percent ascorbic acid; and citric acid, 2–5 percent. The plant is herbaceous with a spiral compound leaf arrangement. The roots are fibrous, ending in groups of three horizontal branches, the ends of which may enlarge greatly to form a few to more than 20 tubers of variable shape and size. Many varieties of potatoes have been developed by cross-breeding. These are grouped according to their response to particular growing conditions; or to the purpose or use to which they are best suited.

It might be noted that the potato contributed greatly to the influx of the Irish to the United States during the last mid-century. The economy of Ireland had become dependent upon the popular, durable potato. But a blight caused a disastrous failure of the crop during the years of 1845 and 1846; the resulting famine and disease among the Irish people made them seek another homeland. Near our old home in Wisconsin, there is a beautiful, serene cemetery dotted with the gravestones of these brave persons who, surprisingly, arrived before the Germans, to what is now a predominantly German area, where sauerkraut and knackwurst are commonly served with the beloved Irish potato. This seems to me to be an outstanding example of two cultures living together in harmony.

DEHYDRATING:
Select firm, smooth potatoes, keeping in mind the purpose for which they will be used, i.e., new red potatoes will not mash satisfactorily, but are good used for salads, frying, or just peeled and generously spread with butter. Steam-blanch, boil or bake the potatoes until they are partially cooked. When the potatoes are cool enough to handle, cut them into 1/2-inch slices or cubes. Immediately place the sliced or cubed potatoes on aluminum (energized) screens and put them into the pyramid, approximately 1 inch above the level of the King's Chamber.

If necessary, use the portable racks of drying screens, and roll the entire stack into the pyramid. The drying time will depend upon the variables in different geographic locations. Put the dehydrated potatoes into airtight plastic or glass containers, or into plastic bags, tightly sealed. Store in a cool, dry, dark place.

TO RECONSTITUTE:

Reconstitute by using the ratio of approximately 2 cups of water to 1 cup of dehydrated potatoes. Pour the water over the potatoes, allow to stand until reconstituted, and then drain. The potatoes may also be reconstituted by dropping them into boiling water and simmering until tender. Drain well. Use the ratio of approximately 3 cups of water to 1 cup of dehydrated potatoes.

USES OF DEHYDRATED POTATOES:

The potatoes reconstituted by either of the above methods can be prepared in many ways. The most familiar:

1. The cooked potato may be served as is with butter, gravy, or seasoning, as desired.

2. Add milk, butter and salt to the cooked potato and mash.

3. Put the cooked potato through a potato ricer.

4. Fry with any additions: bacon, onions, etc.

5. The dehydrated cooked or raw potatoes may be used in soups, chowders, stews, or casseroles.

6. Use the dehydrated cooked potatoes for hot potato salad, or for any other potato recipe of your choice.

SCALLOPED POTATOES

Ingredients:
3   cups reconstituted raw potatoes
1   cup whole milk
2   tablespoons butter
1   teaspoon Worcestershire sauce

1   teaspoon salt
Grated cheese, Parmesan or cheddar

Procedure:
    Butter casserole well. Put potatoes in casserole. Heat milk. Add butter, Worcestershire sauce and salt to milk and pour the mixture over the potatoes. Sprinkle cheese over top, cover and bake in 375° F. oven for 30 minutes. Remove cover and continue baking until potatoes are tender, and the top is lightly browned.
    If reconstituted cooked potatoes are used for this recipe, shorten the baking time until all ingredients are thoroughly blended together and the top is browned.

MASHED POTATO PATTIES

Ingredients:
2   cups cold mashed potatoes
1   tablespoon reconstituted onions
1   teaspoon reconstituted parsley flakes
1   egg
1   tablespoon flour
1   teaspoon salt

Procedure:
    Beat egg, mix with remaining ingredients and shape the mixture into small patties. Sauté in butter until brown and crisp on both sides.

Mushrooms

    There are many different types of mushrooms—edible and nonedible. Both can be found in the wild state, but extreme caution must be taken in identifying the poisonous varieties. Many good books are available that contain color photographs of the various types that make correct identification possible. However, if there is any question about those that are edible, *don't use them.* Seek the advice of your local county agriculture agent who is trained in mushroom identification.

The type most often used are commercially grown varieties known as the Bisporus, which consists of a stem (stipe) and a cap (pileus). While mushrooms have only limited food value, they have been prized by gourmets for centuries because of their delicate taste and texture.

A 100-gram serving (about 3-1/2 ounces) contains 17 calories, 2 grams protein, a trace of fat and 2 grams carbohydrate.

DEHYDRATING:

Select fresh, firm mushrooms. Soak them in well-salted water to aid in cleaning. Rinse well and cut off the

Drying mushrooms

tips of the stems. Discard any woody stems or inferior mushrooms. Cut mushrooms in 1/4-inch slices and steam-blanch until well heated through. Drain and spread cut sections on energized aluminum screen wire about 1 inch above the King's Chamber level. Drying time will depend on the variables in different geographic locations. Place dehydrated mushrooms in a glass or plastic airtight container and store in a cool, dark place.

TO RECONSTITUTE:

Mushrooms dehydrate to approximately 1/4 their original size, so use sufficient water in reconstituting to bring them back to normal size. For use in any recipe requiring long cooking such as stews or soups, the mushrooms can be dropped without reconstitution directly into cooking kettle.

Mushrooms are so widely used in the culinary arts that it is difficult to select recipes for inclusion here. However, these are some typical formulas:

SAUTÉED MUSHROOMS

Ingredients:
2   cups drained reconstituted mushrooms
2   tablespoons butter
Salt to taste

Procedure:

Melt butter in frying pan. Add well-drained mushrooms and salt. Cook slowly about 20 minutes, turning occasionally with a wooden spoon. Serve over hot buttered toast. Sautéed mushrooms are a fine accompaniment to steak, any beef cut, or folded into an omelet.

MACARONI AND MUSHROOMS

Ingredients:
2   cups reconstituted mushrooms

1   cup cream
1   tablespoon melted butter
1/2 pound macaroni (cooked)
1/2 cup grated mild cheddar cheese
1/4 cup reconstituted onions
Salt and white pepper to taste
Buttered bread crumbs

Procedure:

Spread butter over bottom of baking dish. Combine the mushrooms, onions and cheese. First, put a layer of cooked macaroni in bottom of dish, then alternate layers of the mushroom mixture and macaroni until the dish is filled. The last layer should be macaroni. Season the cream with salt and pepper to taste and pour it over the contents of the dish. Sprinkle buttered bread crumbs over the top. Bake in moderate oven at 350° F. for about 30 minutes.

CHICKEN WITH MUSHROOMS AND TOMATOES

Ingredients:
2   cups dehydrated mushrooms
1-1/2 cups dehydrated chicken
1/8 cup butter or olive oil
1/4 cup dehydrated onions
1   6-ounce can tomato paste
3   cups water or chicken broth
1   bay leaf

Procedure:

Bring water or broth to a boil. Add all above ingredients to liquid. Simmer until tender, adding more water or broth as needed. Season to taste.

Beans

There are a number of different types of beans

grown in the United States. They are leguminous plants adsorbing nitrogen from the atmosphere and conducting it to the clusters of nodules on the root system where it is converted to plant food.

The importance of the four varieties, i.e., green, lima, soy and common (which includes kidney, pinto, etc.), can be shown by the volume grown in the United States annually: Soy beans about 465,000,000 bushels, common beans—14,300,000 CWT., green beans fresh—1,500,000 CWT., and green beans for canning and freezing—335,000,000 tons.

Here in the western part of the United States pinto beans (common) are an important staple in the diet—to a great extent replacing the potatoes. This popularity probably stems from the fact that early settlers had to carry foodstuffs that had high nutritional value, were light to carry and were not perishable. To this day the standard meal at roundup time on the big cattle ranch is still steak broiled over a mesquite fire, pinto beans and boiled coffee. As the cowboys say "that sticks to the ribs."

A 100-gram portion (about 3-1/2 ounces) of common beans contains 90 calories, 6 grams protein, trace of fat and 16 grams carbohydrate.

A 100-gram portion (about 3-1/2 ounces) of lima beans contains 111 calories, 7 grams protein, trace of fat and 20 grams carbohydrate.

A 100-gram portion (about 3-1/2 ounces) of green beans contains 25 calories, 2 grams protein, trace of fat and 5 grams carbohydrate.

DEHYDRATING:

Shell beans and spread in a single layer on energized aluminum screen wire trays placed about 1 inch above the King's Chamber level. If a large amount of beans is to be dehydrated and the pyramid is small, use multiple trays. Spread the beans on the trays and stack them, placing a tray with casters on the bottom. Roll the entire stack into the pyramid. Drying time will depend upon the variables in different geographic locations. Store in plastic bags, sealed tightly, or in airtight glass or plastic containers. Following are some typical formulas for reconstituting and using dried beans:

FRIJOLES

Ingredients:
2   cups dehydrated pinto beans
Water

Procedure:
Wash and clean pinto beans and place in a heavy covered saucepan. Cover with water and cook slowly until beans are very tender (approximately 3 hours). If during cooking the liquid becomes low, always add boiling water, and do not salt until about halfway through the cooking process. The beans may be served as they are, or just before serving add a tablespoon of smoking hot pure lard and 1/4 cup of shredded mild cheese.

To serve refritos or refried beans, mash the cooked beans, add the hot lard and cheese, mix well. Serve as soon as the cheese has melted.

BAKED LIMA BEANS

Ingredients:
2   cups dehydrated lima beans
6   cups water
1/2   cup dehydrated onion
1   clove dehydrated garlic (chopped)
1   tablespoon prepared mustard (hot mustard preferred)
1   teaspoon Worcestershire sauce
1   teaspoon salt
2   tablespoons vinegar
2   tablespoons brown sugar
1/4   pound salt pork, ham or bacon cut into pieces

Procedure:

Soak dehydrated lima beans overnight in cooking kettle. Add salt, onions and garlic to the beans. Cover, and simmer until tender, adding more hot water if necessary. Drain, allowing a small amount of liquid to remain. Add remaining ingredients. Put into casserole, cover and bake in a 325° F. oven for one hour.

Green Beans

Select tender beans. Wash carefully, snip off ends and leave whole or cut as desired. Steam-blanch until thoroughly heated through. Drop in cold water to cool; drain, or pat dry with paper towels. Spread green beans evenly in a single layer on energized aluminum screen wire tray and place about 1 inch above the King's Chamber level. If the pyramid is outdoors and is made of a translucent material, such as fiberglass, the bright rays of the sun may bleach the color from the beans. Cover trays that are exposed to the sun with a nonfading porous black gauze. Black crepe paper may be used, but it must be slightly elevated from the trays to prevent the black color from bleeding onto the damp beans. Drying time will depend on the variables in different geographic locations. Store in plastic bags, tightly sealed, or in airtight glass or plastic containers in a cool, dark place.

TO RECONSTITUTE:

Green beans may be reconstituted by covering with a double amount of cold water. Or they can be quickly reconstituted by dropping into boiling water and cooking until tender.

The following is a formula for using dehydrated green beans:

GREEN BEANS WITH BACON AND ONIONS

Ingredients:
2   cups dehydrated green beans

1/4   cup dehydrated onions (cubed)
2-4   slices of diced bacon
4   cups water
Salt to taste

Procedure:
    Place all ingredients in saucepan and cover with water. Bring to a boil and simmer gently until vegetables are tender. Do not let the mixture cook dry, but add extra water if needed. Salt to taste. Dehydrated potatoes may be added about halfway through the cooking time if desired. If potatoes are added, increase the water accordingly. This was a satisfying, favorite recipe from my German-oriented mother's kitchen.

Parsley

    The parsley used in our kitchens is a hardy, biennial herb of the carrot family native to Mediterranean lands. The clusters of dark green tender leaves were used by the ancient Greeks and Romans as a flavoring and garnish for foods, as they are now used in European and American modern times. Parsley dehydrates easily, and can be used either reconstituted or in the dried state.

DEHYDRATION:
    Wash parsley carefully, discarding any inferior leaves. Tie the stems together in clusters and hang, stem end up, in the pyramid. Or the leafy tops can be snipped from the stems. Spread evenly on energized aluminum screen trays and place to dry 1 inch above the King's Chamber level. Drying time will depend on the variables in different geographic locations. Store dehydrated parsley in tightly sealed glass or plastic containers.

TO RECONSTITUTE:
    The parsley can be reconstituted by placing in cold

141

water, or it can be used dry by crumbling the crisp leaves off the stems.

Celery Leaves

Celery is a hardy, biennial plant, and like parsley, native to the Mediterranean area, and first used by the Greeks and Romans. For use in the formulas in this book, the celery tops can be dehydrated in the same manner as parsley.

DEHYDRATION:
Wash the celery tops thoroughly, tie with a string, and hang in clusters in the pyramid. Or the leafy tops can be cut in small pieces, spread evenly on energized aluminum screen trays and placed to dry 1 inch above the King's Chamber level. Drying time will depend on the variables in different geographic locations. Store dehydrated celery leaves in tightly sealed glass or plastic containers.

TO RECONSTITUTE:
The dehydrated celery leaves can be reconstituted by placing in cold water, or they can be used dry by crumbling for use in soups and stews.

DEHYDRATING FRUITS

Apples

It has been said that "an apple a day keeps the doctor away," but this subject we are not qualified to comment on. We do know that apples are an excellent food and can be prepared in a number of ways.

Generally speaking, varieties that mature and are

Dehydrating fruit, from left to right, apples, peaches, and pears

harvested in the summer do not have good keeping qualities. The later the harvest the better, short of freezing temperatures, of course. If apples are kept just above the freezing point (apples freeze at 28.5° F.), the storage life will be longest. But this presents a problem because they are bulky and take up a lot of space. Dehydration can be the answer. And apples dry nicely in the pyramid.

A 100-gram portion (about 3-1/2 ounces) of apple contains 58 calories, trace of protein, trace of fat and 15 grams of carbohydrate.

DEHYDRATING:

Peel and core apples. Slice into 1/4-inch wedges. Make up a solution of 4 tablespoons salt to 1 gallon water. Dip slices of apples in solution to prevent discoloration. Drain and spread out on absorbent toweling to

143

remove excess water. Pat dry, being careful not to bruise slices. Distribute slices over surface of energized aluminum screen wire and place about 1 inch above King's Chamber level. If necessary, use the multiple screen drying trays, and roll the stack into the pyramid. Drying time will depend on the variables in different geographic locations. Like all dehydrated foods, apples should be stored in airtight containers in a cool, dark place.

Following are some typical formulas for using dehydrated apples.

Apples can be eaten as a dried snack food or reconstituted by placing in water, wine or fruit juice.

APPLE CRISP

Reconstitute apples by placing in cold water.

Ingredients:
4   cups sliced apples
1   teaspoon lemon juice
1/3   cup sifted flour
1   cup rolled oats
1/2   cup brown sugar
1/2   teaspoon salt
1   teaspoon cinnamon
1/3   cup melted butter

Procedure:
Spread the sliced apples on the bottom of a well-buttered baking dish. Sprinkle 1 teaspoon lemon juice over apples. Combine flour, rolled oats, brown sugar, salt, cinnamon and melted butter, and sprinkle over apples. Bake at 375° F. for 30 minutes.

APPLE TORTE

Ingredients:
1   cup chopped reconstituted apples

1   egg (well beaten)
3/4   cup sugar
1/2   cup flour
1   teaspoon baking powder
1/8   teaspoon salt
1/2   cup chopped walnuts
1/4   teaspoon cinnamon

Procedure:
Mix sugar into beaten egg. Sift together flour, baking powder and salt. Fold into egg and sugar mixture, add apples, nuts and cinnamon. Pour into well-greased pan and bake for 40 minutes in a 350° F. oven. Serve with whipped cream.

Pears

Pears are the second most important commercial deciduous crop, next to apples, grown in the United States. About 90 percent of the crop is grown in California and Washington.

Pears are more delicate than apples and do not store as well. The commercial practice is to store them at 34° F. at which temperature they will not ripen. When ripe pears are needed in the produce section of stores, the temperature is increased to 60° F. at which point they are ripe. Even then, however, the most popular commercial varieties will keep well for only six to eight weeks when stored at 34° F. This relatively short storage period under refrigeration, plus the space required, makes dehydration all the more attractive.

A 100-gram portion (about 3-1/2 ounces) of pears contains 63 calories, 1 gram protein, a trace of fat and 15 grams carbohydrate.

DEHYDRATING:
To dehydrate pears, follow the instructions for dehy-

145

drating apples. Be sure to store in airtight containers to prevent moisture picked up from the atmosphere. Place in airtight containers in a cool, dark place.

Following are some typical formulas for using dehydrated pears. Pears can be eaten dried as a snack food or they can be reconstituted by placing in water, wine or fruit juice.

PEAR PIE

Reconstitute pears by placing in cold water.
Ingredients:
4   cups reconstituted sliced pears (approximately 2 cups dehydrated)
1/2   cup sugar
3/4   teaspoon cinnamon
1-1/2 tablespoons flour
1   tablespoon butter

Procedure:
Prepare pastry for two 8-inch pie crusts. Combine sugar, cinnamon and flour. Mix lightly through pears. Place into pastry-lined pan. Dot with butter. Cover with top crust, through which slits have been cut. Seal and flute. Bake at 425° F. for 10 minutes. Lower oven temperature to 350° F. and continue baking for 45 minutes, or until pears are tender when tested with a toothpick.

Peaches

Thousands of varieties of peaches (almond family) have been developed worldwide over many centuries. Of these, about 300 varieties are, or have been, grown in the United States. The most popular are: Elberta, Carman, Belle and Greenstone.

The principal producing regions in North America

146

are along the Atlantic coast, foothill districts of Georgia and Alabama, southern Illinois, Michigan, Colorado, eastern Texas, California, Washington and Oregon.

Peaches are subject to insect pests; the most serious is the borer. Fortunately this can be controlled. (See formulas in the section devoted to garden pests.)

A 100-gram portion (about 3-1/2 ounces) of peaches contains 38 calories, 1 gram protein, trace of fat and 10 grams carbohydrate.

DEHYDRATING:

To dehydrate peaches, follow the instructions for apples. Dip in salt solution to prevent discoloration. Store in airtight containers.

Following are some typical formulas for using dehydrated peaches. Peaches are an excellent snack food or they can be reconstituted by placing in water, wine or fruit juice.

PEACH COBBLER

Reconstitute peaches by placing in cold water.
Ingredients:
3   cups reconstituted peaches
1   cup sugar
1   cup water
1   cup flour
1   tablespoon sugar
1-1/2 teaspoons baking powder
1/2   teaspoon salt
3   tablespoons shortening
1/2   cup milk
3   tablespoons cornstarch

Procedure:
Mix 1/2 cup sugar and cornstarch. Gradually stir in

cold water. Bring to a boil and boil for 1 minute, stirring constantly. Add fruit. Pour into a 1-1/2 quart dish. Dot with butter. Sprinkle 1 teaspoon cinnamon over fruit. Combine flour, remaining sugar, baking powder and salt. Cut in shortening. Drop by spoonfuls on hot fruit. Bake at 375° F. for 25 to 30 minutes. Serve warm with cream.

SPICED PEACHES

Ingredients:
6   cups reconstituted peaches
1   cup vinegar
1   cup honey
3   whole cloves
3   sticks cinnamon

Procedure:
Mix vinegar, honey, cloves and cinnamon in saucepan. Heat to a simmer. Add peaches. Cool and chill for several hours. Drain. Serve spiced peaches with ham.

Dehydrating Chicken

It is suggested that the chicken be cooked before it is put into the pyramid for dehydration. Not only will the chicken be readily available for use at home, but if you have a hunter, camper or backpacker in your family, it will be a bonanza. After a long day when the body is weary and the stomach empty, your outdoor person will be able to prepare a piping hot, flavorsome meal within 15 minutes.

Wash the chicken well, cutting it up or leaving it whole. Sprinkle with salt and rub with a small amount of dehydrated onion or garlic. Place the chicken into a heavy covered roasting pan and bake it in a 350° F. oven approximately 1 hour or until it is tender. The purpose of the oven cooking is to retain within the chicken as many of the juices as possible. When cool enough to handle, discard skin, remove chicken meat from bones and put in refrigerator to cool. When thoroughly cooled, spread the chicken in single layers on the aluminum (energized) screen drying trays in the pyramid where they will be slightly above the level of the King's Chamber. Drying time will depend upon the variables in different geographic locations. Put the dehydrated chicken into sealable plastic bags or into airtight glass or plastic containers. Store in a cool, dry place.

TO RECONSTITUTE:

1. Dehydrated chicken may be reconstituted by mixing it with whatever other foods it will be cooked with, adding sufficient liquid, and simmering all slowly until tender.

2. Drop the chicken into boiling water; simmer until reconstituted. Retain the liquid in which the chicken has been simmered. Keep in freezer. It will be ready for soups, stews or chowders.

The following recipes are typical formulas for preparing dehydrated chicken:

CHICKEN SOUP

Ingredients: (1 or 2 servings)

2	cups chicken broth or water
1/2	cup dehydrated chicken
1/4	cup dehydrated carrots
1	tablespoon dehydrated onions
1	teaspoon dehydrated parsley
1	teaspoon celery tops
1/4	cup quick cooking rice

Procedure:

Bring liquid to a boil. Add remaining ingredients and simmer slowly, adding more water if needed, until all ingredients are reconstituted and tender. Season to taste with salt and pepper.

CHICKEN CHOWDER

Ingredients: (1 or 2 servings)
2   cups water
3/4   cup dehydrated chicken
1/4   cup dehydrated carrots
1/4   cup dehydrated green beans
1/4   cup dehydrated potatoes
1   tablespoon dehydrated onions
1   teaspoon dehydrated parsley

Procedure:
   Bring water to a boil. Add remaining ingredients, simmer slowly, adding more water if needed, until all ingredients are reconstituted and tender. Season to taste with salt and pepper.
   These recipes may be altered to suit the number and the tastes of persons to be served. Experiment by adding whatever dehydrated vegetables you may have on hand.

DEHYDRATING MEAT AND FISH

   If you enjoy outdoor activities such as hunting, fishing, camping, backpacking, hiking and skiing—or if you recognize the possibility of blackouts and catastrophes that can cause power failures, beef jerky should be in your larder.
   Beef jerky was made and eaten by many people before the advent of refrigeration. Beef, and some other meats as well, were dried over fires, while the American Indians hung their beef in the sun to dry. History tells us that wagon trains on their long trek from east to west would dry slabs of meat on the canvas tops of the wagons to help keep the people supplied with food.
   A 100-gram portion (about 3-1/2 ounces) of dried beef contains 203 calories, 34 grams protein, 6 grams fat and no carbohydrates.

DEHYDRATING:

The procedures for pyramid dehydrated beef are somewhat different from those for vegetables and fruits. Fats are not easily removed by pyramid energy. Therefore, it is important to choose cuts that are as lean as possible, such as round steak. And then, remove all visible fat that can be cut off.

The slices of beef to be dehydrated should be about 1/4-inch thick, cut into strips about 1 inch wide and 6 inches to 8 inches long for easy storage in a sealed airtight jar.

After the strips have been cut and excess fat removed, they should be well seasoned with salt and pepper, plus any additional dry condiments that suit your taste, such as onion powder or salt, garlic powder, etc.

Because meat will shrink appreciably as it dries, we

Beef jerky

prefer to cure it in a press to minimize the distortion. Using a regular clean energized aluminum surface (used for dehydrating fruits and vegetables), the strips should be placed on the screen. Next, another screen and frame should be inverted so that it sandwiches the meat between the two screen surfaces. Now, secure the two upward and downward screens so the beef is held securely in place. Dehydration time will depend on the variables in different geographic locations. Store in airtight glass or plastic containers in a cool, dark place. Jerky is excellent as a tasty, nourishing snack food.

Making Venison, Elk and Moose Jerky

Generally speaking, wild meats are easier to dehydrate than domestic ones because of the lower fat content.

The same procedures used in making beef jerky may be followed for wild game.

Dehydrating Fish

Like beef jerky, fish was dried and widely used by the early settlers and American Indians before the days of mechanical refrigeration. The drying procedures were taught to the settlers by the Indians.

DEHYDRATING:

Lean fish dehydrate best in the pyramid. Since most of the oil is found directly under the skin, the fish should be skinned rather than scaled. The next step is to filet and cut the filets into strips about 1/4-inch thick and to any length that's suitable. Wash and dry well. Salt and pepper to taste. The drying process should begin immediately due to the delicacy of fish.

Place cut strips on energized aluminum screen 1 inch

above the King's Chamber level. Next, another frame and screen should be inverted and placed on the strips so that the fish is sandwiched between the two screens. Now secure the upper and lower screens so the fish is held securely in place to prevent distortion during the drying process. If a large amount of fish is to be dehydrated and the pyramid is small, use multiple drying screen trays and roll the entire stack into the pyramid. Provide for ventilation as shown for the miniature pyramid. Dehydrate the fish until it is all thoroughly dried. Drying time will depend on the variables in different geographic locations. Be sure to check for spoilage. Place dehydrated fish in sealable plastic bags or in airtight glass or plastic containers. Store in a cool dark place.

There are many different varieties of fish that can be dehydrated. Therefore, in giving values an average has been used.

A 100-gram serving (about 3-1/2 ounces) of fish contains about 200 calories, 20 grams protein, 10 grams fat and 2 grams of carbohydrate. The following recipes are some typical formulas for reconstituting and using pyramid dehydrated fish:

FISH CHOWDER

Reconstitute fish in cold water.
Ingredients:
1-1/2 lbs. reconstituted fish
2   cups dehydrated potatoes
1/2 cup dehydrated onions
3   tablespoons butter
1   cup cream
5   cups water

Procedure:
Mix the fish, potatoes and onions together. Add salt and pepper to taste, and 5 cups water. Simmer gently un-

til ingredients are tender. Add butter and 1 cup of cream and allow to simmer for 5 more minutes.

FISH CAKES

Reconstitute dehydrated fish by boiling.

Ingredients:

1   cup cold boiled flaked fish
1   cup cold mashed potatoes
1   egg (beaten)
1   tablespoon reconstituted onions
1   teaspoon dehydrated parsley flakes or celery top
      flakes used as they are. Both may be used.

Procedure:

Mix fish, potatoes, onions, celery and/or parsley flakes and season with salt and pepper to taste. Add beaten egg and mix thoroughly. Mold into patties and fry in butter, turning until both sides are brown.

DEHYDRATING PLANTS AND FLOWERS

All types of flowers, leaves, grasses and weeds dry beautifully in the pyramid. They are conducive to interesting decorations that last indefinitely when not subjected to rough handling.

There are no special instructions needed as the standard procedures outlined in the food dehydration section apply here as well. There is, however, a method for holding the stems which has not been previously explained.

Most of us have seen the rigid white plastic foam that florists use for flower arrangements. This material is excellent for holding flowers in an upright position while they dry. It is inexpensive to buy and can be used many times over.

Drying plants in styrofoam inside the pyramid

PYRAMID YOGURT

Yogurt is a food with high nutritional value used in many countries of the world. In the United States cow's milk is the principal ingredient, while in central Europe, sheep and goat's milk are used. In southeastern Europe, Egypt and India water buffalo milk is extensively used.

The conventional method of making yogurt is to sterilize the milk and then add a small batch of a previous culture. The mixture is then held at about 112° F. to 115° F. until a curd develops. Thus, it is a product of fermentation.

While we have no idea what causes milk to change to yogurt in the pyramid without the addition of a starter, we know from a considerable amount of experience that it does. And, after all, that's "the proof of the pudding." (No pun intended.)

155

Yogurt on left was made in a pyramid. Soured milk on right stood for same length of time without refrigeration outside of pyramid.

The procedure is simple. Milk, either whole, 2 percent fat or skimmed, can be put into the pyramid in suitable containers. The conversion to yogurt takes about 20 hours. The finished product should then be chilled before eating; store in refrigerator.

A 100-gram portion (about 3-1/2 ounces) of yogurt contains about 65 calories, about 4 grams protein, 2 grams fat and 6 grams carbohydrates.

Following are some interesting formulas for making and using yogurt:

PLAIN YOGURT

Ingredients:
1   quart Grade A, 2 percent or skimmed milk
Salt to taste

Procedures:

Put milk in large-mouth container and place jar at King's Chamber level in pyramid. Do not disturb. After about 20 hours the curd will form, leaving a layer of whey (very thin watery liquid with a bluish cast) over the surface of the curd. Strain off this liquid and salt yogurt to suit, stirring well. Pack seasoned yogurt into containers and store in refrigerator.

VARIATIONS OF PLAIN YOGURT

1. Fruit juices alone, or in combination with their fruit, may be mixed with the finished plain yogurt. These include: strawberries, raspberries, blackberries, boysenberries, apples, pears, peaches, apricots, oranges, lemons, limes, etc.

2. Yogurt may be flavored in any number of ways including syrups such as chocolate, butterscotch, maple, etc. Also extracts may be used including almond, vanilla, wintergreen, mint, etc.

BACKPACKING

Few sports have enjoyed the phenomenal surge of popularity by kids and adults alike that backpacking has. And no wonder.

Many folks have become so accustomed to zooming down the road in their Belchfire V8 gas guzzlers that "seeing" what is going on is impossible. But when you walk, a whole new world of sights, sounds and scents opens up. A red squirrel or jaybird scolds from a tree daring you to invade their domain. The drumming sound in the distance that sounds like an old "one lunger" gas engine is a partridge (grouse) dancing for its would be mate on the courting log.

Next, the hiker can be in for a real experience if he/she will find an ant hill. Sit next to it on a log and watch the show. A constant single file procession of ants will be hauling food in and debris out, which may include dead ants among other things. But the dead ants are never dropped around the rim of the mound as other objects may be. Rather, they are dragged away and deposited in a remote location. And if you're lucky you may see their "court in session." This consists of a ring of ants, with those on trial in the center. Now one of two things will happen. Either the ranks will break and the accused are free, or the ants will converge and kill the guilty ones, dragging them away. These are just a few of the many miraculous things to be seen if we walk and observe. But walking takes energy, and energy can only be supplied by food.

The experienced backpacker knows (and the novice soon learns) that an ounce at the beginning of the hike can feel like a pound halfway up that next hill. So the name of the game is: keep the weight to a minimum.

Most undried foods contain at least 75 percent water. This means that for every pound you carry only four ounces is available for supplying energy. And, of course, undried foods spoil quickly because the bacteria require water to do their "dirty work." So dehydrated foods are the answer. And those dried with pyramid energy contain no artificial preservatives and taste much better than the ones dried commercially. Here are some suggestions for using pyramid dehydrated foods for that next backpacking trip.

SNACKS

We think the best dehydrated foods to eat along the way between meals are meats and fruits. Meat, such as beef jerky for example, is high in protein and swells in the stomach averting hunger pangs. Pyramid dried apples, pears and peaches are delicious to munch on, and are high in natural fruit sugar which supplies almost instant energy. And, they replace the desire for candy which we all know is harmful to children's teeth.

For recipes refer to dried fruits, jerky, and dehydrated chicken formulas.

CAUTION TO READERS

In dehydrating food, utmost care should be taken to see that conditions are clean from start to finish. Wash hands often with soap and water. Don't handle food if you have sores on your face, hands, or arms. Keep tables, counters, cutting surfaces, knives, and other equipment scrupulously clean. Shield foods from insects at all times.

The efficacy of your pyramid in dehydration may depend on the temperature and humidity conditions in the area in which it is situated. Sustained heat and low humidity are the best conditions for drying foods. Cooler temperatures coupled with low humidity are the next best conditions. In areas of normally high humidity pyramid drying may be done in only a limited way, when favorable conditions exist. If drying takes more than thirty-six hours the possibility of mold is increased.

The safe maximum percentages of water to leave in home-dried produce are no more than 5 percent for vegetables and no more than 20 percent for fruit. You may therefore do a weight check for dryness. Ten ounces of fresh vegetables should weigh one-half ounce when fully dried. Ten ounces of fruit should weigh two ounces when fully dry.

Always check dehydrated food particularly meat and other proteins both before and after storage to be certain there is no mold or infestation, no off odor, and no rancidity. Any foods that show any of these properties should be immediately discarded!

Index

Index

Index

Norman Stark, author of the bestsellers *The Formula Book* and *The Formula Book 2*, holds over a dozen patents on his inventions, many with America's leading corporations. His work in chemistry goes back to 1940, when he founded the Stark Research Corporation to conduct research, development, and manufacturing in the chemical field. Stark's work in the field of chemistry has required considerable expansion; he established his own laboratory in Tucson, Arizona, for analyzing existing products, creating new formulas, and undertaking thorough testing of each of his formulas.

Stark's interest in pyramids began after doubting the unusual powers that archeologists and researchers were ascribing to pyramids. He now operates over a half dozen pyramids at his Tucson laboratories, including a scale model of the famous Cheops pyramid, which stands on a 20 foot base and is 12 feet high.

The Formula Book, derived from his textbook *The Formula Manual,* has enjoyed tremendous success with over 200,000 copies in print; *The Formula Book 2,* with over 75,000 copies in print. Stark is also the author of a nationally syndicated column, "The Formula," which appears in over 100 newspapers.

Other Popular Books from Sheed Andrews and McMeel, Inc.

Wine Is the Best Medicine
By Dr. E. A. Maury $6.95 (cloth)
The Formula Book
By Norman Stark $10.00 (cloth); $5.95 (paper)
The Formula Book 2
By Norman Stark $10.00 (cloth); $5.95 (paper)
The Formula Book 1 and 2 Slipcased Gift Pack
By Norman Stark $11.90 (paper)
Oven Drying: The Best Way to Preserve Foods
By Irene Crowe $5.95 (cloth)
Good Earth Almanac A to Z Dictionary of Health Food Terms
By Michael Balfour and Judy Allen $2.95 (paper)
Good Earth Almanac Old Time Recipes
By Mark Gregory $1.95 (paper)
Good Earth Almanac Natural Gardening Handbook
By Mark Gregory $1.95 (paper)
Good Earth Almanac Survival Handbook
By Mark Gregory $1.95 (paper)
All the Things Your Mother Never Taught You
By Charlotte Slater $4.95 (paper)
Things Your Mother Never Taught You About Car Care and Repair
By Charlotte Slater $2.50 (paper)

If you are unable to obtain these books from your local bookseller, they may be ordered from the publisher. Enclose payment with your order.

Sheed Andrews and McMeel, Inc.
6700 Squibb Road
Mission, Kansas 66202